Praise For
The Jewish
& Informatio

D0803768

"This is a remarkable book. It is amazing how much non-trivial information the author included in these impressive, enlightening pages."
—**Dr. Philip Birnbaum,** author and translator
The Daily Prayer Book,
The High Holyday Machzor,
The Abridged Mishneh Torah

"A delightful book filled with not-so-trivial information."
—**Blu Greenberg,**
President, JWB Jewish Book Council,
author of *How To Run a Traditional Jewish Household*

"Ian Shapolsky's JEWISH TRIVIA & INFORMATION BOOK offers both education and recreation. It is a book not only to read but to also play—a treasure between covers."
—**M. Hirsch Goldberg,** author of
The Jewish Connection,
Just Because They're Jewish,
The Blunder Book,
The Book Of lies

"THE JEWISH TRIVIA & INFORMATION BOOK is an easy and enjoyable way to become well informed about every aspect of Jewish life."
—**Rabbi Alfred J. Kolatch,** author of
The Jewish Book of Why
The Second Jewish Book of Why

- On the *B'nai B'rith Jewish Monthly Bestseller List* for over ten months.

- The bestselling Jewish paperback in America.

- Over 100,000 copies in print.

THE NEW
JEWISH TRIVIA
&
INFORMATION
BOOK

✡

IAN SHAPOLSKY

S.pi
BOOKS
A Division Of Shapolsky Publishers

The New Jewish Trivia & Information Book

S.P.I. BOOKS
A division of Shapolsky Publishers, Inc.

ISBN 1-56171-175-6

For any additional information, contact:

S.P.I. BOOKS/Shapolsky Publishers, Inc.
136 West 22nd Street
New York, NY 10011
212/633-2022 / FAX 212/633-2123

Manufactured in Canada

10 9 8 7 6 5 4 3 2 1

DEDICATION

For my parents, Anita and Meyer,
whose help was appreciated,

For my sister Lisa, and her family,
For my grandparents and their family,

For Annie and her family.

I.S.

ACKNOWLEDGEMENTS

I would like to sincerely thank the various librarians in the Judaica departments of the New York City libraries I visited in the course of completing this project. They graciously offered countless hours of their time and guided me to the research materials crucial to the success of this endeavor.

In the event that any errors or misinterpretations occur in these pages, I alone bear full responsibility.

In addition, THE NEW JEWISH TRIVIA & INFORMATION BOOK owes its greatest debt to you the readers who purchased the first JEWISH TRIVIA & INFORMATION BOOK. Your support inspired me to do the hard but fulfilling work of searching out and compiling the thousands of new questions that were the source material for this edition.

I am indebted to the many kind readers and eminent Jewish scholars who sent me their ideas for improving this book and who assisted in identifying existing questions-and-answers in the first edition that may have needed further clarification.

Hopefully, this printing will be totally free of errors. But if not, I await and encourage your letters pointing out corrections and your suggested new questions.

Ian Shapolsky
New York City, 1994

INTRODUCTION

Readers often ask why I call this series "JEW-ISH TRIVIA & INFORMATION" since there is nothing trivial about Judaism or Jewish history. The reason really is because I thought it was a fun-sounding name for a book that I intended to be fun to read and fun to learn from.

I hope readers do learn from these questions and answers about this rich and extraordinary culture and heritage.

On a more personal level, the writing and researching of THE NEW JEWISH TRIVIA & INFORMATION BOOK has been an exciting, rewarding, informative and stimulating experience. In order to locate the most diverse and entertaining questions, I went through many books, encyclopedias, biographies, newspapers, magazines and journals. Fortunately, Jewish culture and history brims over with such extraordinary people and events that I did not have to search far to find thousands of exceptional questions. The problem became which to use here and which to save for the next volume.

Because of the convenient structure of the questions and answers, this book is especially well suited for use as a quiz or a game among groups of people who consider themselves to be knowledge-able about Jewish topics.

Challenge your friends and family and discover who is best informed on subjects of Jewish interest.

If you, the reader, wish to offer any comments, suggestions or new questions, I would warmly welcome them. If your questions are accepted for the next edition, we will send you a copy of the new book as a gift. Please address all responses to:

THE JEWISH TRIVIA CONTEST
Shapolsky Publishers, Inc.
136 West 22nd Street
New York, New York 10011

Trivia Judaica　　QUESTIONS

CURRENT
EVENTS　1.　➤ What is a dangerous aspect of the 1994 "peace progress" with the P.L.O. which is being ignored by Israeli negotiators but which will have major quality-of-life implications for many geographic areas in Israel. . . ?

WOMEN　2.　➤ This character actress provides the voice of Marge Simpson on *The Simpsons*. Her name is. . .?

ARTS &
CULTURE　3.　➤ What was Jewish writer Neil Simon's most successful play. . . ?

PEOPLE　4.　➤ During the years prior to the Holocaust, this Zionist leader prophetically warned Europe's Jews to "Liquidate the exile before the exile liquidates you . . ."?

RELIGION　5.　➤ Why are autopsies not permitted under Jewish law?

HISTORY　6.　➤ This famous trial began in Jerusalem on April 11, 1961 and ended on May 31, 1962, when the accused was found guilty and hanged. . .?

LANGUAGE 7.　➤ In Germany, what word was inscribed on the yellow stars that the Nazis forced all Jews to wear . . .?

GEOGRAPHY 8.　➤Ben-Gurion was offered this location, in 1946, for a Jewish homeland . . .?

ANSWERS

CURRENT
EVENTS   **1.** ➤ **The lands Israel will be giving up are the sources of most of Israel's underground water supplies.**

WOMEN   **2.** ➤ **Julie Kavner.**

ARTS &
CULTURE   **3.** ➤ **The Odd Couple. (It was so popular it was made into a T.V. series).**

PEOPLE   **4.** ➤ **Vladimir (Ze'ev) Jabotinsky.**

RELIGION   **5.** ➤ **Jews take the position that man was created in the image of God. Therefore, the holiness of human beings demand that we do not tamper with them.**

HISTORY   **6.** ➤ **The trial of Adolf Eichmann. (He organized the Nazi extermination program while directing Sub-Department IV 4b of the Reich Security Division).**

LANGUAGE   **7** ➤ *Jude* **(Jew in German).**

GEOGRAPHY   **8.** ➤ **An area in Vietnam was offered by Ho Chi Minh.**

Trivia Judaica   **QUESTIONS**

CURRENT
EVENTS   9.   ➤ What organization sent a speaker to Kean College in New Jersey who made the assertion that "75% of the slaves owned in the South were owned by Jews". . . ?

WOMEN   10. - ➤ In 1972, Sally J. Preisand became the first Jewish woman to . . .?

ARTS &
CULTURE   11.   ➤ This noted film about modern Israel's early history was based on the true story of a U.S. Army Colonel who joined the Israeli Army . . .?

PEOPLE   12.   ➤ Which outrageous former African dictator publicly declared his admiration for Hitler's "Final Solution"?

RELIGION   13.   ➤ The story of Purim begins with a conflict between King Ahashverosh and Queen Vashti. Biblical commentators disagree on Vashti's fate. What are the two main opinions on what happened to her . .?

HISTORY   14.   ➤ Christopher Columbus had this Jewish interpreter on his ship. . .?

LANGUAGE 15.   ➤ *Aliyah* refers to a Jew who migrates to Israel. It means literally . . .?

GEOGRAPHY 16. ➤ This deep sea port is Israel's outlet to Africa and Asia; its subtropical waters make it a major Israeli resort...?

ANSWERS

CURRENT
EVENTS 9. ➤ **The Nation of Isalm. (The speaker was Abdul Muhammed, an aid to Louis Farrakhan.)**

WOMEN 10. ➤ **Be ordained a rabbi (in the American Reform Movement).**

ARTS &
CULTURE 11. ➤ *Cast A Giant Shadow* —**The Story of Colonel David "Mickey" Marcus.**

PEOPLE 12. ➤ **Idi Amin of Uganda.**

RELIGION 13. ➤ **She was either executed or banished from the kingdom.**

HISTORY 14. ➤ **Luis de Torres. (He reportedly attempted to converse in Hebrew with the Indians he met in the New World thinking that they could have been from a lost tribe of Israel.)**

LANGUAGE 15. ➤ **To Ascend.**

GEOGRAPHY 16. ➤ **Eilat.**

CURRENT
EVENTS   17. ➤ Political and military experts speculate
that Israel has at least 100 of these special
powerful items?

WOMEN   18. ➤ This American Jewish movie actress, who
dated Henry Kissinger, was born Jill
Oppenheim. . .?

ARTS &
CULTURE   19. ➤ Which Academy-Award winning screen-
writer created advertisements criticizing
the Allies for refusing to rescue Jews from
Hitler during the War years?

PEOPLE   20. ➤ In 1985, the Congressional Gold Medal of
Achievement was presented to this Jewish
professor who writes about the Holocaust
. . .?

RELIGION 21. ➤ The walls of Jericho collapsed after this
kind of horn was blown how many
times. . .?

HISTORY   22. ➤ This Israeli war followed a period of de-
ceptive calm, during which the Arab states
discreetly reorganized and rebuilt their
military power . . .?

LANGUAGE 23. ➤ What does the Moslem word *Jihad* mean?

GEOGRAPHY 24. ➤ Before 1967, how many miles wide was
Israel at its narrowest point?

ANSWERS

CURRENT
EVENTS 17. ➤ Nuclear Warheads.

WOMEN 18. ➤ Jill St. John.

ARTS &
CULTURE 19. ➤ Ben Hecht.

PEOPLE 20. ➤ Elie Wiesel.

RELIGION 21. ➤ A ram's horn, blown seven times.

HISTORY 22. ➤ The Six-Day War.

LANGUAGE 23. ➤ A "Holy War" to destroy the Jewish
state.

GEOGRAPHY 24. ➤ Nine miles wide.

Trivia Judaica   **QUESTIONS**

CURRENT
EVENTS   25. ➤ During the Yom Kippur War how close to Damascus did Israeli forces get (within 5 miles accuracy). . .?

WOMEN   26. ➤ She is the Jewish author of *Looking For Mr. Goodbar* and *August* . . .?

ARTS &
CULTURE   27. ➤ What is the stage name of the Jewish, Hungarian-born, actor Lazlo Lowenstein, famous for his sinister characters . .?

PEOPLE   28. ➤ Josephus was not only a talented Jewish General, but also renowned as. . .?

RELIGION   29. ➤ Which two Biblical animals could talk, and to whom did they talk. . .?

HISTORY   30. ➤ The Balfour Declaration was written in the form of a letter to which prominent, Jewish British philanthropist. . .?

LANGUAGE   31. ➤ A General in the Israel Defense Forces is known in Hebrew as . . .?

GEOGRAPHY   32. ➤ The Tower of Babel was supposed to reach this location . . .?

ANSWERS

CURRENT
EVENTS 25. ➤ **25 miles.**

WOMEN 26. ➤ **Judith Rossner.**

ARTS &
CULTURE 27. ➤ **Peter Lorre.**

PEOPLE 28. ➤ **A historian.**

RELIGION 29. ➤ **A snake spoke to Eve; an ass to Balsam.**

HISTORY 30. ➤ **Lord Rothschild.**

LANGUAGE 31. ➤ *Aluf.*

GEOGRAPHY 32. ➤ **Heaven.**

Trivia Judaica   **QUESTIONS**

CURRENT
EVENTS   33. ➤ Name the accused assassin of Rabbi Meir Kahane. . .?

WOMEN   34. ➤ This granddaughter of a *shochet* (ritual slaughterer), a Ph.D. in electrical engineering and a design engineer for RCA, was the first Jewish-American astronaut . . .?

ARTS &
CULTURE   35. ➤ This versatile Jewish author also played the role of architect Stanford White in the movie *Ragtime* . . .?

PEOPLE   36. ➤ He was the U.S. Labor Secretary, the U.S. Ambassador to the U.N., and a U.S. Supreme Court Justice—all within 5 years . . .?

RELIGION   37. ➤ This holiday involves the tradition of sending gifts of food. Also, what is the food called . . .?

HISTORY   38. ➤ Who built the First Temple and royal palace in Jerusalem and made Israel a great nation of traders?

LANGUAGE   39. ➤ What is the woman's section in an Orthodox synagogue called in Hebrew?

GEOGRAPHY   40. ➤ The Dead Sea Scrolls were found in a cave in this city near the Dead Sea . . .?

ANSWERS

CURRENT
EVENTS 33. ➤ **El Sayyid Nossair, one of the partici-pants in the World Trade Center bombing.**

WOMEN 34. ➤ **Judith A. Resnick.**

ARTS &
CULTURE 35. ➤ **Norman Mailer.**

PEOPLE 36. ➤ **Arthur Goldberg.**

RELIGION 37. ➤ **Purim. (The presents are called "*Shalach Manot*").**

HISTORY 38. ➤ **King Solomon (David's son—who ruled from 961 BCE to 920 BCE).**

LANGUAGE 39. ➤ *Ezrat Nashim.*

GEOGRAPHY 40. ➤ **Qumran.**

Trivia Judaica | QUESTIONS

CURRENT
EVENTS 41. ➤ What was the defense strategy in the Demjanjuk trial?

WOMEN 42. ➤ In 1963, what Jewish feminist wrote the classic text of the women's movement, and what was the title of her book?

ARTS &
CULTURE 43. ➤ Jewish artists Jerry Siegel and Joe Shuster created this world-famous comic book character in the 1930's . . .?

PEOPLE 44. ➤ He was the first person born on Earth. . .?

RELIGION 45. ➤ How many days did Jonah spend in the belly of the whale?

HISTORY 46. ➤ On December 11, 1917, this British General led the forces that entered Jerusalem and ended four centuries of Ottoman rule over the Holy Land . . .?

LANGUAGE 47. ➤ Ladino (the Sephardic Jewish language) is a derivation of what two languages?

GEOGRAPHY 48. ➤ Israeli super-spy Eli Cohen operated primarily in this country?

ANSWERS

CURRENT
EVENTS   41. ➤ They claimed it was all simply a case of mistaken identity and the accused was not "Ivan The Terrible".

WOMEN   42. ➤ Betty Friedan, *"The Feminine Mystique."*

ARTS &
CULTURE   43. ➤ Superman.

PEOPLE   44. ➤ Cain.

RELIGION   45. ➤ Three days.

HISTORY   46. ➤ General Allenby (formally known as Viscount Edmund Henry Hyman Allenby).

LANGUAGE   47. ➤ Spanish and Turkish. (It is often mistakenly assumed that Ladino's origin is Hebrew).

GEOGRAPHY   48. ➤ Syria. (He rose to the level of second in command of the Syrian Government.)

Trivia Judaica   **QUESTIONS**

CURRENT
EVENTS   49. ➤ Which ultra-Orthodox party in Israel was rocked by financial scandals in the early 1990's effecting the coalition governments of Likud and Labor. . .?

WOMEN   50. ➤ What was the name of Moses' mother?

ARTS &
CULTURE   51. ➤ He was the evil Jewish character in Dickens' *Oliver Twist*. . .?

PEOPLE   52. ➤ This Jewish financier was a major supporter of the American Revolution . . .?

RELIGION   53. ➤ The destruction of the Temple resulted in these two crises . . .?

HISTORY   54. ➤ On the night of November 9th, 1938, the Nazis burned 191 synagogues, destroyed 815 Jewish shops, and smashed the windows of Jewish homes and stores throughout Germany. That evening came to be known as . . .?

LANGUAGE   55. ➤ What is *chametz*?

GEOGRAPHY   56. ➤ When did large numbers of Jews begin to settle in Eastern Europe?

ANSWERS

CURRENT
EVENTS 49. ➤ The Sephardic *Shas* party.

WOMEN 50. ➤ Yocheved.

ARTS &
CULTURE 51. ➤ Fagin.

PEOPLE 52. ➤ Hayim Salomon.

RELIGION 53. ➤ The Jewish people lost their land and they believed the Divine Presence—the "*shekhina*"—had departed from Jerusalem.

HISTORY 54. ➤ "*Kristallnacht*," or the night of broken glass.

LANGUAGE 55. ➤ Leavened bread, that is not to be seen, eaten, enjoyed or profited from during *Pesach*.

GEOGRAPHY 56. ➤ In the 13th century. (Polish kings wanted business-oriented Jews to help diversify Poland's agricultural economy into a commerce-oriented one.)

CURRENT
EVENTS 57. ➤ How many Jews are there now in Libya, if any. . .?

WOMEN 58. ➤ Women now exceed men at which division of graduate theological studies. . .?

ARTS &
CULTURE 59. ➤ What Jewish movie star/comedian and specialist in crude, self-deprecating humor said, "If it weren't for pickpockets, I'd have no sex life at all"?

PEOPLE 60. ➤ What do Bobby Fisher, Karl Marx, Heinrich Heine and Benjamin Disraeli all have in common?

RELIGION 61. ➤ This Jewish-born leader is the Father of Christianity. What are his English and Hebrew names. . .?

HISTORY 62. ➤ In 1863, the most anti-Semitic act in American history occurred when this U.S. General (and eventual Republican Presidential candidate) ordered all Jews expelled from Tennessee . . .?

LANGUAGE 63. ➤ The last three words of the Passover Seder *Le-shanah Ha-ba-ah B'Yerushalayim* mean . . .?

GEOGRAPHY 64. ➤ During the Jewish exodus from Egypt, what two bodies of water parted?

ANSWERS

CURRENT
EVENTS 57. ➤ **None. The last remaining Libyan Jews were driven out after savage pogroms in 1967.**

WOMEN 58. ➤ **Cantorial.**

ARTS &
CULTURE 59. ➤ **Rodney Dangerfield.**

PEOPLE 60. ➤ **They were all Jews who converted to Christianity.**

RELIGION 61. ➤ **Jesus Christ. (Yehoshua).**

HISTORY 62. ➤ **General Ulysses S. Grant (in his famous General Order #11. President Lincoln immediately revoked this order—when it was brought to his attention).**

LANGUAGE 63. ➤ **Next year in Jerusalem.**

GEOGRAPHY 64. ➤ **The Red Sea and the Jordan River.**

Trivia Judaica   QUESTIONS

CURRENT
EVENTS   65.   ➤ Cite 3 reasons why Israel is so important to Jews who live outside of Israel. . .?

WOMEN   66.   ➤ This Jewish movie maker directed the motion picture *Exodus* . . .?

ARTS &
CULTURE   67.   ➤ He is the non-Jewish conductor of the Israeli Philharmonic . . .?

PEOPLE   68.   ➤ These two well-known Canadian Jewish entrepreneurs own the Montreal Canadians ice hockey team and Seagram's whiskey and beverage company . .?

RELIGION   69.   ➤ Synagogues throughout time have had these three major functions . . .?

HISTORY   70.   ➤ This famous 1916 agreement provided for joint Anglo-French-Russian control of all parts of Palestine containing holy places. . .?

LANGUAGE   71.   ➤ This Hebrew name for God appears on *mezuzahs*. . .?

GEOGRAPHY   72.   ➤ The Jews of Spain as well as this less publicized country were faced with the decision of death or expulsion if they did not convert to Christianity . . .?

ANSWERS

65. ➤ 1. The Bible refers to it as the land of the Jewish people.

2. Jews have lived in various parts of the land of Israel continuously since the beginning of time, so they have a historic claim to the land.

3. There is so much latent anti-Semitism, Jews cannot be certain conditions where they live will not worsen to the point that they will prefer to leave—for Israel.

4. The Holocaust demonstrated that massive genocide against the Jews was acceptable to the world and even under these horrendous conditions, few countries granted Jews asylum, therefore having a country of one's own is important.

WOMEN 66. ➤ Otto Preminger.

ARTS &
CULTURE 67. ➤ Zubin Mehta.

PEOPLE 68. ➤ Edgar and Peter Bronfman.

RELIGION 69. ➤ A house of assembly (*Beth Ha Keneseth*), a house of study (*Beth Ha Midrash*), and a house of prayer (*Beth Ha Tefillah*).

HISTORY 70. ➤ The Tripartite (Sykes-Picot) Agreement of 1916.

LANGUAGE 71. ➤ *Shaddai*

GEOGRAPHY 72. ➤ Portugal

Trivia Judaica **QUESTIONS**

CURRENT
EVENTS 73. ➤ These new Israeli immigrants protested against the Chief Rabbinate's ruling that they undergo "conversion" to Judaism by means of immersion in a *mikvah*, the Jewish ritual bath . . .?

WOMEN 74. ➤ This noted Biblical woman, the subject of a Book of the Bible, was a convert to Judaism. . .?

ARTS &
CULTURE 75. ➤ This Jewish heroine parachuted into Hungary during the Holocaust in order to rescue Jews, but was captured and tortured to death by the Nazis . . .?

PEOPLE 76. ➤ He was prime minister of Israel during the 1956 Sinai Campaign . . .?

RELIGION 77. ➤ The explanation for Jews being "chosen people" is based on this principle . . .?

HISTORY 78. ➤ He was the first of the five Jewish Justices of the U.S. Supreme Court . . .?

LANGUAGE 79. ➤ What is *Gematria*?

GEOGRAPHY 80. ➤ This country's National Bank admitted in a recent study, that it had helped to finance the Nazi war-machine during World War II by accepting gold stolen by the Nazis from Jews and the treasuries of occupied counties . . .?

ANSWERS

CURRENT
EVENTS **73.** ➤ **The Ethiopian Jews. (Israel's chief Rabbis initially could not agree on the Jewish status of the Ethiopian Jews. Shortly after this controversy erupted, they protested and this procedure was abolished.)**

WOMEN **74.** ➤ **Ruth.**

ARTS &
CULTURE **75.** ➤ **Hannah Senesh.**

PEOPLE **76.** ➤ **David Ben-Gurion.**

RELIGION **77.** ➤ **That they had an ethical role to play through the practice of their religion.**

HISTORY **78.** ➤ **Louis D. Brandeis.**

LANGUAGE **79.** ➤ **A mystical method of explaining Hebrew words according to the numerical value of the individual letters. (Known today as numerology.)**

GEOGRAPHY **80.** ➤ **The Swiss National Bank. (The study was written by a former archivist of the Swiss banking system.)**

Trivia Judaica   QUESTIONS

CURRENT
EVENTS   81.   ► Investigation into the World Trade Center bombing reopened consipracy charges for what previous crime against a Jew. . .?

WOMEN   82.   ► This American Jewish author wrote *Generation Without Memory* the story of her personal Jewish awakening . . .?

ARTS &
CULTURE   83.   ► In 1635, this legendary non-Jewish artist painted "Abraham's Sacrifice". . .?

PEOPLE   84.   ► Which leader of the Jewish underground in pre-state Israel assumed the name "Rabbi Israel Sassover," when he hid from the British . . .?

RELIGION   85.   ► This seminary trains American Reform rabbis and was founded in Cinncinnati by Isaac Mayer Wise . . .?

HISTORY   86.   ► What was embarrassing to the U.S. government about the post World War II activities of Nazi war criminal Klaus Barbie. . .?

LANGUAGE   87.   ► This Israeli leader, who recently lost his job, was directly involved with the following political controversies: building a stadium near Sanhedria Marhevet, fighting against the Ramat Road demonstrators and destroying the illegally built synagogue in Gilo. . .?

GEOGRAPHY   88.   ► These Israeli ruins are known as the "Castle of the Pilgrims. . .?"

ANSWERS

CURRENT
EVENTS   81. ➤ The assassination of Rabbi Meir Kahane.

WOMEN   82. ➤ Ann Roiphe.

ARTS &
CULTURE 83. ➤ Rembrandt.

PEOPLE   84. ➤ Menachem Begin. (During his Stern
gang years.)

RELIGION 85. ➤ Hebrew Union College.

HISTORY 86. ➤ He was employed by the American government from 1947 to 1950 in the U.S.
Counter-Intelligence Corps. (It has also
been alleged that U.S. officials gave him
false identity papers so he could avoid
earlier arrest attempts.)

LANGUAGE 87. ➤ Former Mayor Teddy Kollek of Jerusalem.

GEOGRAPHY 88. ➤ "Atlit." (They are on the coast, just
south of Mt. Carmel.)

Trivia Judaica QUESTIONS

CURRENT
EVENTS 89. ➤ What joint operation did the C.I.A., the State Departmeat and the U.S. Air Force conduct in the mid-1980's that was of significance to the entire Jewish world?

WOMEN 90. ➤ This former Jewish wife of Cary Grant was born Samile Diane Friessen . . .?

ARTS &
CULTURE 91. ➤ This best-selling gentile author recently wrote a second book on Jewish Americans entitled *The Rest of Us* . . .?

PEOPLE 92. ➤ Born Lev Davidovich Bronstein, this Bolshevik revolutionary played a key role in the Communists' seizure of power in Russia. In 1940, he was murdered by his rivals in the Soviet hierarchy . . .?

RELIGION 93. ➤ Philadelphia's Liberty Bell monument has the following inscription: "Proclaim liberty throughout all the land unto all the inhabitants thereof." It is a quote from this book of the Old Testament . . .?

HISTORY 94. ➤ In this year, Israel was admitted as a member to the United Nations . . .?

LANGUAGE 95. ➤ *Fedayeen* is the Arab word which means. . .?

GEOGRAPHY 96. ➤ The 1985 hijacking of TWA flight 847 occured at this international airport. . .?

ANSWERS

CURRENT
EVENTS 89. ➤ **They coordinated the successful Ethiopian Jewish rescue mission.**

WOMEN 90. ➤ **Dyan Cannon. (Cary was born Jewish, but hid it most of his life.)**

ARTS &
CULTURE 91. ➤ **Stephen Birmingham (who also wrote "*Our Crowd*").**

PEOPLE 92. ➤ **Leon Trotsky.**

RELIGION 93. ➤ **Leviticus.**

HISTORY 94. ➤ **1949—May 11. (Statehood was achieved on May 14, 1948, but it took an additional year to formalize entry into the United Nations.)**

LANGUAGE 95. ➤ **"Men of sacrifice."**

GEOGRAPHY 96. ➤ **Athens International Airport.**

Trivia Judaica **QUESTIONS**

CURRENT
EVENTS 97. ➤ Which Israeli political party was banned from elections for being "Nazi-like, undemocratic and racist". . .?

WOMEN 98. ➤ This Jewish movie actress played leading roles in *Terms of Endearment*, *An Officer and A Gentleman* and *Shadowlands*. . .?

ARTS &
CULTURE 99 ➤ This Pulitzer Prize-winning Jewish photographer took the famous photo of six marines raising the American flag at Iwo Jima. . .?

PEOPLE 100. ➤ These five Jewish lawyers served as Justices on the U.S. Supreme Court . . .?

RELIGION 101. ➤ Born in Paris to Polish Jewish immigrants, Aaron Lustiger is renowned for having risen to which high position within the Roman Catholic Church . . .?

HISTORY 102. ➤ Spanish Jew Luis De Torres acted as an interpreter for this noted explorer in what year . . .?

LANGUAGE 103 .➤ What Hebrew song is sung on Friday night, at the onset of the Sabbath . . .?

GEOGRAPHY 104.➤ The Jews of India, living primarily in Bombay and Cochin, call themselves by this name. . .?

ANSWERS

CURRENT
EVENTS 97. ➤ **Rabbi Kahane's *Kach* party.**

WOMEN 98. ➤ **Debra Winger.**

ARTS &
CULTURE 99. ➤ **Joe Rosenthal.**

PEOPLE 100. ➤ **Benjamin Cardozo, Louis Brandeis, Arthur Goldberg, Abraham Fortas, and Felix Frankfurter.**

RELIGION 101. ➤ **The Catholic Archbishop of Paris. (His new name is Jean Marie Cardinal Lustiger. He was protected by gentiles during the war and assumed a Christian identity to survive—and must have liked it.)**

HISTORY 102. ➤ **Christopher Columbus. (Torres was a Marrano, expelled from Spain in 1492— the same year Columbus set sail).**

LANGUAGE 103. ➤ **"*Lecha Dodi.*"**

GEOGRAPHY 104. ➤ **Bene Israel (House of Israel).**

CURRENT
EVENTS   105. ➤ What person involved in the Watergate
                scandal said, "Those Jewboys are every-
                where. You can't stop them."

WOMEN   106. ➤ These two Jewish comediennes became
                famous after their roles in the series *Satur-
                day Night Live* . . .?

ARTS &
CULTURE   107. ➤ The Jewish actor famous for his cowboy
                roles, had a number-one hit record called
                Ringo, in 1964 . . .?

PEOPLE   108. ➤ This famous Zionist leader suggested the
                establishment of a Jewish homeland in
                Uganda . . .?

RELIGION 109. ➤ Who was the very first Jewish sailor, re-
                ferred to repeatedly in the Bible?

HISTORY   110. ➤ Located in New York City, this world-
                renowned institution was the first Jewish
                hospital in the United States. . .?

LANGUAGE 111. ➤ What is the traditional Yiddish *Shabbos*
                greeting. . .?

GEOGRAPHY 112. ➤ This nation has the largest Jewish popula-
                tion in South America . . .?

ANSWERS

CURRENT
EVENTS 105. ➤ **Richard Nixon (to John Dean).**

WOMEN 106. ➤ **Gilda Radner, Lorraine Newman.**

ARTS &
CULTURE 107. ➤ **Lorne Greene.**

PEOPLE 108. ➤ **Theodor Herzl.**

RELIGION 109. ➤ **Noah.**

HISTORY 110. ➤ **Mount Sinai Hospital. (Today, it is one of the largest and most prestigious medical centers in the world.)**

LANGUAGE 111. ➤ *A gutn Shabbos.*

GEOGRAPHY 112. ➤ **Argentina; current estimates are more than 350,000 Jews.**

Trivia Judaica   **QUESTIONS**

CURRENT
EVENTS   113. ➤ This Jewish public servant was the first
             non-American born to ever hold a U.S.
             Cabinet post. . .?

WOMEN   114. ➤ This female convert to Judaism said, "Your
             people shall be my people, and your God
             my God" . . .?

ARTS &
CULTURE 115. ➤ Professor Gershom Sholem wrote the de-
             finitive biography of this seventeenth Cen-
             tury False Messiah . . .?

PEOPLE   116. ➤ In 1905, this chemist became the first Jew
             ever to win a Nobel Prize. . .?

RELIGION 117. ➤ Perhaps the most renowned Jewish phi-
             losopher of all time, this sage was also a
             famous medical educator who served as
             personal physician to the Sultan of
             Egypt. . .?

HISTORY 118. ➤ This Ireland-born President of Israel at-
             tended Cambridge University and began
             his career in politics as an announcer on
             the BBC . . .?

LANGUAGE 119. ➤ What is *loshan hara*?

GEOGRAPHY 120. ➤ This partially excavated archeological park
             just outside the walls of Jerusalem's Old
             City, was opened to the public in the
             summer of 1985?

ANSWERS

CURRENT
EVENTS 113. ➤ **Henry Kissinger.**

WOMEN 114. ➤ **Ruth (the Moabite).**

ARTS &
CULTURE 115. ➤ **Shabatai Zvi.**

PEOPLE 116. ➤ **Adolph Von Bayer.**

RELIGION 117. ➤ **Moses Maimonides.**

HISTORY 118. ➤ **Chaim Herzog.**

LANGUAGE 119. ➤ **Literally "evil tongue" meaning slanderous gossip. (Observant Jews are forbidden from engaging in it.)**

GEOGRAPHY 120. ➤ **The City of David Archeological Park.**

Trivia Judaica **QUESTIONS**

CURRENT
EVENTS 121. ➤ The Defense Minister of Israel during the Six-Day War was. . .?

WOMEN 122. ➤ Who was *Lillith* in Jewish myth . .?

ARTS &
CULTURE 123. ➤ He was born Eugene Silverstein and starred with Zero Mostel in Mel Brooks' controversial film *The Producers* . . .?

PEOPLE 124. ➤ Which world conqueror was so kind to the Jews that many named their sons after him?

RELIGION 125. ➤ Which Biblical Commandment is considered a "double *mitzvah*" if performed on the Sabbath?

HISTORY 126. ➤ This Jewish doctor who attended to England's King Richard, was also a Rabbi and a Philosopher . . .?

LANGUAGE 127. ➤ The word *Yiddishkeit* means . .?

GEOGRAPHY 128. ➤ The "Good Fence" crossing point between Israel and Lebanon is located in this northern Israeli town.

ANSWERS

CURRENT
EVENTS 121. ➤ **Moshe Dayan.**

WOMEN 122. ➤ **Adam's brazenly self-centered female counterpart before the creation of Eve.**

ARTS &
CULTURE 123. ➤ **Gene Wilder.**

PEOPLE 124. ➤ **Alexander the Great.**

RELIGION 125. ➤ **Sexual relations between husband and wife.**

HISTORY 126. ➤ **Moses Maimonides.**

LANGUAGE 127. ➤ **Jewishness.**

GEOGRAPHY 128. ➤ **Metulla.**

Trivia Judaica   **QUESTIONS**

CURRENT
EVENTS   129. ➤ What distinguishes the Jerusalem Zoo and
                   its unusual collection of animals from all
                   other zoos around the world . .?

WOMEN   130. ➤ The *New York Times* called this Nobel
                   laureate in medicine "'The Madame Curie
                   from the Bronx". . .?

ARTS &
CULTURE   131. ➤ The "Avenue of the Righteous Gentiles" is
                   located on the grounds of this world fa-
                   mous Jerusalem institution . . .?

PEOPLE   132. ➤ This famous Israeli soldier once declared,
                   "Better to keep Sharm el-Sheikh and not
                   have peace with Egypt, than to surrender
                   Sharm el-Sheikh and have peace" . . .?

RELIGION   133. ➤ This sinful act, according to the Talmud, is
                   equivalent to murdering three people . . .?

HISTORY   134. ➤ This War was the outcome of an Arab
                   policy, announced four years earlier, to
                   weaken and destroy Israel. . .?

LANGUAGE 135. ➤ What does the Hebrew, *Am-haretz* mean?

GEOGRAPHY 136 ➤ The United States has been Israel's pri-
                   mary arms supplier since 1973. From which
                   country did Israel acquire most of its weap-
                   ons during the 1950's and 1960's. . .?

ANSWERS

CURRENT
EVENTS   129. ➤ **It only houses animals that are referred to in the Bible.**

WOMEN   130. ➤ **Rosalyn Sussman Yalow.**

ARTS &
CULTURE   131. ➤ **Yad Vashem (Israel's memorial to the victims of the Holocaust).**

PEOPLE   132. ➤ **Moshe Dayan.**

RELIGION   133. ➤ **Slanderous gossip. (The three victims are the speaker, the listener, and the person who was slandered.)**

HISTORY   134. ➤ **The 1956 Sinai War.**

LANGUAGE   135. ➤ **An ignorant Jew; a Jew who has little or no knowledge of Judaism.**

GEOGRAPHY   136. ➤ **France.**

Trivia Judaica　　QUESTIONS

CURRENT
EVENTS　137. ➤ On June 7, 1981, Israeli planes attacked,
and destroyed this objective deep inside
Arab territory. . .?

WOMEN　138. ➤ Israel's Conservative and Reform semi-
naries achieved what milestone in 1993?

ARTS &
CULTURE　139. ➤ This non-Jewish composer and lyricist
once said to his Jewish friend Richard
Rogers, "The secret of my success is that I
write Jewish tunes". . .?

PEOPLE　140. ➤ This Jewish physicist discovered radio
waves, and their unit of measurement is
named after him. . .?

RELIGION　141. ➤ Among assimilated American Jews, this
religious ritual above all others has become the most widely observed . . .?

HISTORY　142. ➤ In 1893, this Zionist leader once suggested
in frustration that the solution to the "Jewish question" was the mass conversion of
Jewish children to Christianity. . .?

LANGUAGE 143. ➤ What does *Galut* mean . . .?

GEOGRAPHY144. ➤ During the Yom Kippur War, this was the
only European nation which granted refu-
eling rights to U.S. aircraft?

ANSWERS

CURRENT
EVENTS 137. ➤ **An Iraqi Nuclear reactor.**

WOMEN   138. ➤ **Both ordained their first woman Rabbi in Israel.**

ARTS &
CULTURE 139. ➤ **Cole Porter.**

PEOPLE 140. ➤ **Heinrich Hertz (as in mega-hertz).**

RELIGION 141. ➤ **Lighting Chanukah candles.**

HISTORY 142. ➤ **Theodor Herzl. (This was documented in his personal diary. He quickly changed his mind.)**

LANGUAGE 143. ➤ **Exile, or the condition of the Jewish people in dispersion.**

GEOGRAPHY 144.➤**Portugal.**

Trivia Judaica   QUESTIONS

CURRENT
EVENTS   145. ➤ What makes Israel politically unique in the Middle East. . .?

WOMEN   146. ➤ What ritual obligation can a man perform only if no woman is available?

ARTS &
CULTURE   147. ➤ He was the first Jewish artist that the Vatican ever commissioned. . .?

PEOPLE   148. ➤ The *Ba'al Shem Tov* was famous for founding this movement in 18th century Poland. . .?

RELIGION   149. ➤ Which books of the Bible were the Ethiopian Jews in possession of during their isolation from the rest of world Jewry?

HISTORY   150. ➤ Later to become the President of a majr Arab state, he was jailed in 1942 by the British for collaborating with the Nazis. . .?

LANGUAGE   151. ➤ *Knaidlach*—a favorite Jewish dish—is known in English as. . .?

GEOGRAPHY   152. ➤ This inland sea is wholly within Israel's borders. . .?

ANSWERS

CURRENT
EVENTS   145. ➤ It is the only Democracy.

WOMEN   146. ➤ Lighting the Sabbath candles.

ARTS &
CULTURE   147. ➤ Marc Chagall. (He made stained glass
                     windows for a large Vatican hall).

PEOPLE   148. ➤ Hasidism.

RELIGION   149. ➤ The first Five Books of Moses, the Book
                     of Joshua and the Book of Ruth.

HISTORY   150. ➤ Anwar Sadat.

LANGUAGE   151. ➤ Matzah Balls.

GEOGRAPHY 152. ➤ Lake Kinneret (also called the Sea of
                     Galilee).

CURRENT
EVENTS 153. ➤ This Jewish writer, professor and lecturer spoke the now famous words "That place, Mr. President, is not your place. Your place is with the victims." Also, who did he speak them to . . .?

WOMEN 154. ➤ In 1903, Jewish female labor activist, Rose Schneiderman, helped to organize this type of group for workers in the garment industry . . .?

ARTS &
CULTURE 155. ➤ In the early 1800's, this German Jewish writer asserted: "Judaism is not a religion but a misfortune" . . .?

PEOPLE 156. ➤ This Zionist leader founded the *Haganah*, the first independent Jewish fighting force in modern times . . .?

RELIGION 157. ➤ In preparation for this holiday, many Ashkenazi Jews decorate their synagogues and homes with flowers, shrubbery and foliage, while many Sephardic Jews decorate their temple Scrolls with floral arrangements . . .?

HISTORY 158. ➤ This leading Israeli statesman was opposed to the 1981 Israeli raid on Iraq's nuclear bomb factory . . .?

LANGUAGE 159. ➤ This word means grandfather in Yiddish . . .?

GEOGRAPHY 160. ➤ The "Damascus Gate" of Jerusalem's old city leads to which quarter of the city. . .?

ANSWERS

CURRENT
EVENTS **153.** ➤ **Elie Wiesel, publicly urging President Reagan not to visit the German military cemetery at Bitburg.**

WOMEN **154.** ➤ **A union. (It was called the United Cloth, Hat, Cap and Millinery Workers Union. She was also President of the Womens Trade Union League from 1926 to 1949.)**

ARTS &
CULTURE **155.** ➤ **Heinrich Heine (who acted on his own dumb advice and converted to Christianity).**

PEOPLE **156.** ➤ **Vladimir Ze'ev Jabotinsky.**

RELIGION **157.** ➤ *Shavuos.*

HISTORY **158.** ➤ **Shimon Peres.**

LANGUAGE **159.** ➤ *Zeydeh.*

GEOGRAPHY **160.** ➤ **The Moslem quarter.**

Trivia Judaica   **QUESTIONS**

CURRENT
EVENTS   161. ➤ Which four non-Arab countries sent troops to aid the Arabs in the Yom Kippur War?

WOMEN   162. ➤ This Jewish television personality, famous for her interviews, originally had the family name of Volters before she went to Hollywood. . .?

ARTS &
CULTURE   163. ➤ Naftali Herz Imber composed this poem in 1878. It was later set to music and became the anthem of the Zionist movement. What is it?

PEOPLE   164. ➤ In 1897, Hungarian-Jewish inventor David Schwarz, was asked by the German government to test his experimental revolutionary transportation device. He died before the test and the device is now known by the name of the German who perfected it . . .?

RELIGION   165. ➤ Maimonides wanted Judaism to be based primarily on this principle . . .?

HISTORY   166. ➤ What did the Jordanians do to the Mount of Olives cemetery when they occupied Jerusalem . . .?

LANGUAGE   167 ➤ The accusation that Jews use the blood of Christians for their religious rites, particularly in the preparation of unleavened bread for Passover, is referred to as . . .?

GEOGRAPHY 168. ➤ This Arab nation has the largest Jewish population?

ANSWERS

CURRENT
EVENTS   161. ➤ Pakistan, Cuba, North Vietnam, and North Korea.

WOMEN   162. ➤ Barbara Walters.

ARTS &
CULTURE   163. ➤ *"Hatikvah"*, Israel's national anthem.

PEOPLE   164. ➤ The Zeppelin (a blimp with a rigid metal frame, that should really be called the Schwarz).

RELIGION   165. ➤ Reason.

HISTORY   166. ➤ They built a hotel over the graves of Jewish sages—desecrating the tomb stones.

LANGUAGE   167. ➤ Blood libel.

GEOGRAPHY 168. ➤ Morocco (over 15,000 Jews).

Trivia Judaica QUESTIONS

CURRENT
EVENTS 169. ➤ Israel has three major intelligence gathering organizations—one is similar to the C.I.A., another is equivalent to the F.B.I., the last branch deals with. . .?

WOMEN 170. ➤ In her last acting role, Ingrid Bergman played this famous Jewish woman . . .?

ARTS &
CULTURE 171. ➤ This Czech-born German Jewish novelist is the author of *The Trial*, *The Castle*, and *Amerika*. After his death, he was recognized as a major figure in European literature . . .?

PEOPLE 172. ➤ This Jewish thinker was the father of modern psychology. . .?

RELGION 173. ➤ One of the most significant developments of this Biblical book is the centralizing of the priestly functions in the family of Aaron and the Levites. . .?

HISTORY 174. ➤Only this superpower showed sympathy for the Zionist movement before World War I, giving serious consideration to Theodor Herzl's 1902 plea that Jewish development of the Sinai Peninsula be facilitated . . .?

LANGUAGE 175. ➤ When non-Jews organize together to have a good time by murdering Jews and destroying Jewish property, this act is often referred to as a . . .?

GEOGRAPHY 176. ➤ This place was the first taste of America for many European Jews. . .?

ANSWERS

CURRENT
EVENTS 169. ➤ **Military Intelligence, (it handles the gathering of information on Arab armies; providing daily analyses of political developments for Government leaders).**

WOMEN 170. ➤ **Golda Meir.**

ARTS &
CULTURE 171. ➤ **Franz Kafka.**

PEOPLE 172. ➤ **Sigmund Freud.**

RELIGION 173. ➤ **Deuteronomy.**

HISTORY 174. ➤ **Great Britiain**

LANGUAGE 175. ➤ **A pogrom. (The organized killing of Jews.)**

GEOGRAPHY 176. ➤ **The Ellis Island Immigration Center.**

Trivia Judaica   QUESTIONS

CURRENT
EVENTS   177. ➤ Name the retired Cleveland auto worker
                  accused of being "Ivan the Terrible". . .?

WOMEN   178. ➤ What ritual observance have women ral-
                  lied around at the Western Wall to assert
                  their right to assemble and pray as
                  women. . .?

ARTS &
CULTURE   179. ➤ This Jewish actor-comedian was the oldest
                  person ever to receive an Academy Award
                  for Best Supporting Actor . . .?

PEOPLE   180. ➤ This chemical in the periodic table is named
                  in honor of a great Jewish scientist. . .?

RELIGION   181. ➤ The partition separating men and women
                  in an Orthodox synagogue is called a . . .?

HISTORY   182. ➤ Biographers claim that newspaper colum-
                  nist Theodor Herzl first conceived the idea
                  of Zionism after covering this infamous
                  trial . . .?

LANGUAGE   183. ➤ Amen, the word stated after all prayers by
                  Jews, is derived from a Hebrew word that
                  in English means...?

GEOGRAPHY   184. ➤ The first kibbutz in Israel, established in
                  1909 on the south shore of Lake Kinneret,
                  was called?

ANSWERS

CURRENT
EVENTS   177. ➤ John Demjanjuk.

WOMEN   178. ➤ Celebration of the New Moon, a traditionally female symbol.

ARTS &
CULTURE   179. ➤ George Burns.

PEOPLE   180. ➤ Einsteinium.

RELIGION 181. ➤ *"Mechitza."*

HISTORY   182. ➤ The Alfred Dreyfus trial (in France).

LANGUAGE 183. ➤ Belief.

GEOGRAPHY 184. ➤ Degania.

Trivia Judaica QUESTIONS

CURRENT
EVENTS   185. ➤ What Harvard professor was dismissed
from stewardship of the Dead Sea Scrolls
because of his anti-Semitic remarks. . .?

WOMEN   186. ➤ This Jewish female entertainer has a mythi-
cal best friend—whom she dislikes—called
Heidi Abromowitz?

ARTS &
CULTURE   187. ➤ This famous Jewish songwriter and composer was born Israel Baline?

PEOPLE   188. ➤ What is the German Jewish philosopher
Martin Buber remembered for. . .?

RELIGION   189. ➤ What renders a bird not kosher?

HISTORY   190. ➤ This ancient Hebrew's revolt resulted in a
short period of Jewish independence and
statehood?

LANGUAGE 191. ➤ The term *shoah* refers to...?

GEOGRAPHY 192. ➤ After Jerusalem fell to the Romans, this
city became a center for Talmudic study
and the location of the Sanhedrin—the
highest religious-legal tribunal of the ancient Jews . . .?

ANSWERS

CURRENT
EVENTS 185. ➤ John Strugnell.

WOMEN 186. ➤ Joan Rivers.

ARTS &
CULTURE 187. ➤ Irving Berlin.

PEOPLE 188. ➤ He was a Mystic.

RELIGION 189. ➤ All birds of prey, such as eagles, are not kosher.

HISTORY 190. ➤ The Bar Kochba Revolt (in 133 C.E.).

LANGUAGE 191. ➤ The Holocaust. It literally means "terrible catastrophe."

GEOGRAPHY 192. ➤ Tiberias.

Trivia Judaica QUESTIONS

CURRENT
EVENTS 193. ➤ In late 1993, these two Jewish comedic authors had the number one and two best-selling books on the *N.Y. Times* list. . .?

WOMEN 194. ➤ Elizabeth Taylor converted to Judaism and had two Jewish husbands named. . .?

ARTS &
CULTURE 195. ➤ These musical Jewish brothers were the most successful American musical comedy producers of their time. . .?

PEOPLE 196. ➤ This controversial American journalist and playwright was a supporter of the *Irgun Zvie Leumi* . . .?

RELIGION 197. ➤ Of the 613 *mitzvot* (commandments), how many are positive commandments . . .?

HISTORY 198. ➤ In 1839, this Englishman proposed the idea of establishing a Jewish State . . .?

LANGUAGE 199, ➤ What is the English translation for the Yiddish expression *prinsesen* . . .?

GEOGRAPHY 200. ➤ Where is the lowest body of water on earth. . .?

ANSWERS

CURRENT
EVENTS   193. ➤ Howard Stern and Jerry Seinfeld

WOMEN   194. ➤ Eddie Fisher and Mike Todd.

ARTS &
CULTURE   195. ➤ The Shuberts.

PEOPLE   196. ➤ Ben Hecht. (Because he strongly be-
                        lieved that the American Jewish estab-
                        lishment was not doing enough to assist
                        the rescue of Europe's Jews during and
                        after World War II.)

RELIGION   197. ➤ 248.

HISTORY   198. ➤ Sir Moses Montefiore.

LANGUAGE   199. ➤ A prima donna or princess.

GEOGRAPHY   200. ➤ The Dead Sea (1312 feet below the level
                        of the Mediterranean Sea).

CURRENT
EVENTS   201. ➤ The only non-Caribbean nation which refused to condemn the United States invasion of Grenada was . . .?

WOMEN   202. ➤ What is the name of the Jewish feminist magazine which calls itself "The Jewish Women's Magazine"?

ARTS &
CULTURE   203. ➤ Shylock's daughter was named. . .?

PEOPLE   204. ➤ As a youth, this former Jewish Cabinet Secretary worked in a shaving-brush factory during the day and attended New York's City College at night . . .?

RELIGION   205. ➤ Why are two loaves of *challah* traditionally found on the Sabbath table?

HISTORY   206. ➤ Israel's "Law of Return" grants automatic citizenship to new Jewish immigrants. In what year was it enacted. . . .?

LANGUAGE   207. ➤ *Mitzvah* literally means . . .?

GEOGRAPHY 208. ➤ The 1956 Arab-Israeli conflict erupted due to the blockade of this waterway. . .?

ANSWERS

CURRENT
EVENTS 201. ➤ Israel.

WOMEN 202. ➤ *Lilith.*

ARTS &
CULTURE 203. ➤ Jessica.

PEOPLE 204. ➤ Henry Kissinger.

RELIGION 205. ➤ To symbolize the double portion of *"Manna"* that was sent by God to feed the wandering Israelites on the Sabbath.

HISTORY 206. ➤ 1950.

LANGUAGE 207. ➤ Commandment (not charity or good deed as many thinks).

GEOGRAPHY 208. ➤ The Straits of Tiran (off the Gulf of Eilat).

Trivia Judaica   **QUESTIONS**

CURRENT
EVENTS   209. ➤ What did Iraq threaten to do to Israel before the Gulf War broke out. . .?

WOMEN   210. ➤ This Jewish writer was the well known restaurant critic for *The New York Times* and wrote numerous guides to fine eating. . .?

ARTS &
CULTURE   211. ➤ The pastry *Hamentaschen* is eaten on what Jewish holiday?

PEOPLE   212. ➤ This American Jewish mobster applied for Israeli citizenship in 1971, and was rejected. . .?

RELIGION   213. ➤ This Biblical figure is the hero of Deuteronomy. He transmits the Divine word, is a prophet, and intermediary, and an advocate for the Jewish people . . .?

HISTORY   214. ➤ The Egyptians were able to bomb Tel Aviv during only one war with Israel. Which war was it?

LANGUAGE   215. ➤ The often used phrase *Eretz Yisrael* means . . .?

GEOGRAPHY   216. ➤ The small Jewish towns of Eastern Europe in which most Jews lived until the 20th Century were called. . .?

ANSWERS

CURRENT
EVENTS   209. ➤ To "burn half of Israel" with chemical weapons.

WOMEN   210. ➤ Mimi Sheraton.

ARTS &
CULTURE   211. ➤ Purim.

PEOPLE   212. ➤ Meyer Lansky.

RELIGION   213. ➤ Moses.

HISTORY   214. ➤ In 1948, during the War of Independence. (At this time, Israel had no effective air defenses).

LANGUAGE 215.➤ The Land Of Israel.

GEOGRAPHY 216.➤ *Shtetls.*

Trivia Judaica   QUESTIONS

CURRENT
EVENTS   217. ➤ How many days did it take for Saddam's forces to conquer Kuwait. . .?

WOMEN   218. ➤ This German-born American political and social philosopher lived in France, and escaped to the U.S. in 1941. Her learned and provocative works include *The Origins of Totalitarianism* and *Eichmann in Jerusalem* ...?

ARTS &
CULTLURE 219. ➤ This Jewish songwriter and musician worked as an accompanist and arranger for Marlene Dietrich. He also composed many popular hits including the musical, *Promises, Promises* and the Oscar-winning score for the movie *Butch Cassidy and The Sundance Kid*. . .?

PEOPLE   220. ➤ Which Jewish doctor and social scientist wrote *The Interpretation of Dreams*. . .?

RELIGION 221. ➤ What was the most radical of the reforms called for by the first Society of Reform Jews in America?

HISTORY 222. ➤ How many times has Israel captured, and then later surrendered, southern Lebanon?

LANGUAGE 223 ➤ What is a *minhag?*

GEOGRAPHY 224 ➤ Albert Einstein was offered the presidency or which country in 1952?

ANSWERS

CURRENT
EVENTS 217. ➤ Two.

WOMEN 218. ➤ Hannah Arendt.

ARTS &
CULTURE 219. ➤ Burt Bachrach.

PEOPLE 220. ➤ Sigmund Freud.

RELIGION 221. ➤ The use of English during its services (it happened in Charleston, South Carolina).

HISTORY 222. ➤ Three (1948, 1978 and 1982).

LANGUAGE 223. ➤ A custom or tradition

GEOGRAPHY224.➤ Israel (He graciously turned down the offer).

Trivia Judaica **QUESTIONS**

CURRENT
EVENTS 225. ➤ The Temple Mount riot of 1990 occurred on what Jewish holiday when the Western Wall plaza was full of worshippers. . .?

WOMEN 226. ➤ This female director and writer was Mike Nichols' first comedy partner . . .?

ARTS &
CULTURE 227. ➤ Which German Jewish philosopher of anti-religious thinking said: "Where there is no reverence for the Bible, there can be no true refinement of manners"?

PEOPLE 228. ➤ This Jewish Pulitzer Prize-winning columnist for *The New York Times* was once an aide to President Richard Nixon. . .?

RELIGION 229. ➤ On *Shavuos*, Jews traditionally stay up all night. What is it they do during these hours?

HISTORY 230. ➤ This famous American politician of the Revolutionary War era said: "I will insist that Hebrews have done more to civilize men than any other nation. . .?"

LANGUAGE 231. ➤ What does the word *kippur* in *Yom Kippur* mean?

GEOGRAPHY 232. ➤ In Hebrew the disputed West Bank lands are called *Yehuda* and *Shomron*. What do these names translate to in English?

ANSWERS

CURRENT
EVENTS   225. ➤ **Sukkot.**

WOMEN   226. ➤ **Elaine May.**

ARTS &
CULTURE   227. ➤ **Friedrich Nietzsche.**

PEOPLE   228. ➤ **William Safire.**

RELIGION   229. ➤ **Study *Torah*.**

HISTORY   230. ➤ **John Adams.**

LANGUAGE   231. ➤ **Atonement.**

GEOGRAPHY 232. ➤ ***Judea* and *Samaria*.**

CURRENT
EVENTS   233. ► In 1949, Israel voted to admit this country
                 to the U.N. Recently, it was reported that
                 Israeli military experts are assisting in the
                 construction of their planes, tanks and
                 missiles . . .?

WOMEN   234. ► What famous woman turned into a pillar of
                 salt because she looked back to watch the
                 destruction of Sodom?

ARTS &
CULTURE   235. ► Which Jewish actor from the television
                 series *Star Trek* once studied in the famous
                 Brisk Yeshiva of Skokie, Illinois?

PEOPLE   236. ► Rambam, Maimonides, and Rabbi Moshe
                 ben Maimon are all. . .?

RELIGION   237. ► The *Mishna* and *Gemara* when combined
                 are called . . .?

HISTORY   238. ► Where is Babi Yar and what happened
                 there?

LANGUAGE   239. ► What does *Megillah* mean?

GEOGRAPHY   240. ► After the 1967 Six-Day War, approxi-
                 mately how many times larger was the new
                 area of Jerusalem?

ANSWERS

CURRENT
EVENTS 233. ➤ **The People's Republic of China.**

WOMEN 234. ➤ **Lot's wife.**

ARTS &
CULTURE 235. ➤ **Leonard Nimoy.**

PEOPLE 236. ➤ **Different names for the same famous person, most often referred to as Maimonodes.**

RELIGION 237. ➤ **The Talmud.**

HISTORY 238. ➤ **In Kiev, Russia. More than 30,000 Jews were killed there by the Nazis in 1941. (In the 1980s, the former Soviet Union built a housing project on the site with no memorial to commemorate the massacre.)**

LANGUAGE 239. ➤ **A scroll. The most famous is the Scroll of Esther, which is read on Purim.**

GEOGRAPHY 240. ➤ **Unified Jerusalem was about three times larger than the original mandate.**

Trivia Judaica   **QUESTIONS**

CURRENT
EVENTS 241. ➤ What country has the U.S. blamed for the bombing of Pan Am flight 103 over Lockerbie, Scotland. . .?

WOMEN 242. ➤ This never-married, leading Jewish feminist said, "The surest way to be alone is to get married" . . .?

ARTS &
CULTURE 243. ➤ In which Jerusalem hospital are the famous Chagall windows located?

PEOPLE 244. ➤ Eleazar Ben Yair was a leader of these anti-Roman rebels . . .?

RELIGION 245. ➤ A common Hebrew blessing is to wish someone to live "until 120". Which Biblical figure died at that age?

HISTORY 246. ➤ The transmission of German Hassidism as well as other forms of German Jewish culture to Eastern Europe was largely caused by this recurring event in world history . . .?

LANGUAGE 247. ➤ When does one say *Gut yuntiff*?

GEOGRAPHY 248. ➤ When Britain caught Jews " illegally" immigrating to Palestine during World War II, they were sent to this country for detention . . .?

ANSWERS

CURRENT
EVENTS 241. ➤ Libya. (Although some knowledgeable sources claim the crime was actually directed by Syria.)

WOMEN 242. ➤ Gloria Steinem.

ARTS &
CULTURE 243. ➤ Hadassah Hospital.

PEOPLE 244. ➤ He commanded the Jews of Masada.

RELIGION 245. ➤ Moses.

HISTORY 246. ➤ Anti-Semitic outbreaks that forced thousands of Jews to migrate.

LANGUAGE 247. ➤ When wishing one a good holiday.

GEOGRAPHY 248. ➤ Cyprus.

CURRENT
EVENTS   249. ➤ This Arab country stubbornly refuses, even today, to consider a cease-fire or armistice agreement with Israel — preferring instead to remain in a permanent state of war . . .?

WOMEN   250. ➤ This Jewish rock and roll singer had a string of hits, beginning in 1963 with her "It's my Party" . . .?

ARTS &
CULTURE   251. ➤ This English-Jewish runner and recipient of a gold medal was featured in the movie *Chariots of Fire* . . .?

PEOPLE   252. ➤ He is known as the preeminent "Nazi hunter" . . .?

RELIGION   253. ➤ This Biblical Book is a narrative of the Israelites' many years of wandering in the desert and their eventual conquest of the Promised Land . . .?

HISTORY   254. ➤ This Jewish holiday and the Warsaw Ghetto uprising occurred on the same date. . .?

LANGUAGE 255. ➤ The Hebrew word *Tzaddik* means . . .?

GEOGRAPHY 256. ➤ Twelve percent of American Jews live in these two boroughs of New York City . . .?

ANSWERS

CURRENT
EVENTS 249. ➤ **Iraq.**

WOMEN 250. ➤ **Lesley Gore.**

ARTS &
CULTURE 251. ➤ **Harold M. Abrahams.**

PEOPLE 252. ➤ **Simon Wiesenthal.**

RELIGION 253. ➤ **The Book of Joshua.**

HISTORY 254. ➤ **Passover.**

LANGUAGE 255. ➤ **Righteous.**

GEOGRAPHY 256. ➤ **Queens and Brooklyn.**

CURRENT
EVENTS   257. ➤ On what conditions did Saddam vow to attack Israel. . .?

WOMEN   258. ➤ It has been alleged that Golda Meir "exchanged" this Jewish underworld figure, seeking Israeli citizenship with the U.S. government—in return for additional Phantom jets . . .?

ARTS &
CULTURE   259. ➤ This great Jewish author wrote the Code of Jewish Law known as the *Shulchan Aruch* . . .?

PEOPLE   260. ➤ This Jewish founder of psychoanalysis was born in Vienna in 1856 and died in London in 1939. . .?

RELIGION 261. ➤ *Yizkhor*, the Hebrew prayer for the dead, is recited in most synagogues on the last day of these three festivals . . .?

HISTORY   262. ➤ This fortress-palace near Bethlehem, built by King Herod is called . . .?

LANGUAGE 263. ➤ The Orthodox Zionist movement is popularly referred to by this name . . .?

GEOGRAPHY 264. ➤ In 1929, Arab pogromists murdered sixty-nine Jews in this Jewish holy city . . .?

ANSWERS

CURRENT
EVENTS 257. ➤ **If the U.S. attacked Iraq (He wimped out, however).**

WOMEN 258. ➤ **Meyer Lansky (this was an undocumented charge).**

ARTS &
CULTURE 259. ➤ **Joseph Caro (in the 16th century).**

PEOPLE 260. ➤ **Sigmund Freud.**

RELIGION 261. ➤ *Pesach, Succos,* **and** *Shavous.*

HISTORY 262. ➤ **Herodion.**

LANGUAGE 263. ➤ *Mizrachi.*

GEOGRAPHY 264. ➤ **Hebron.**

CURRENT
EVENTS   265. ➤ What was the code name for the 1981
               Israeli mission to destroy Iraq's nuclear
               reactor . . .?

WOMEN   266. ➤ What national organization did Hannah
               Greenebaum Solomon found . . .?

ARTS &
CULTURE   267. ➤ As Israel's most famous painter, he has
               made original contributions to optic and
               kinetic art. In many of his paintings, the
               picture is changed by the movement of
               either the object or the viewer. . .?

PEOPLE   268. ➤ What was the name of the Jewish inter-
               preter on Columbus' voyage of discovery,
               who was also the first man to set foot in the
               new world. . .?

RELIGION 269. ➤ Identify three major ways in which Reform
               and Orthodox Jews differ in their religious
               practices . . .?

HISTORY   270. ➤ During the 1670's, much of the Jewish
               world was convinced that he was the Mes-
               siah—until he converted to Islam . . .?

LANGUAGE 271. ➤ The Hebrew phrase *Shalom Bayit* means
               . . .?

GEOGRAPHY 272. ➤ The Arab flag was modeled after the flag
               of Nazi Germany . . .?

ANSWERS

CURRENT
EVENTS 265. ➤ Operation Babylon.

WOMEN 266. ➤ She founded the National Council of Jewish Women, the first U.S. national Jewish women's organization.

ARTS &
CULTURE 267. ➤ Yaacov Agam.

PEOPLE 268. ➤ Rodrigo Sanches (There were also other Jews on board).

RELIGION 269. ➤ Any of these: the use of *Tefillin*, the separation of men and women during prayer services, the ritual slaughtering of animals for koshering, and for men to pray with a covered head.

HISTORY 270. ➤ Shabbatai Zvi (The False Messiah).

LANGUAGE 271. ➤ Peace of the household.

GEOGRAPHY 272. ➤ Egypt.

Trivia Judaica　　　　　**QUESTIONS**

CURRENT
EVENTS　273. ➤ In at least three member-states of the Arab League, slavery is still widely practiced. Name one of them. . .?

WOMEN　274. ➤ This overweight Jewish rock singer was born Ellen Naomi Cohen . . .?

ARTS &
CULTURE　275. ➤ This famous Conservative Rabbi's writings are modern classics of Jewish spirituality. He was well known as both an anti-war and civil rights activist. . .?

PEOPLE　276. ➤ This French-Jewish entertainer is considered the world's greatest mime . . .?

RELIGION　277. ➤ This verb appears no fewer than 169 times in the Bible . . .?

HISTORY　278. ➤ This Jewish organization was established in 1922 by the League of Nations' Mandate for Palestine. It was reorganized in 1929 to encourage non-Zionist Jews to provide financial support to create a Jewish homeland. It was in effect a Jewish Government — even before there was a Jewish state . . .?

LANGUAGE 279. ➤ The Hebrew-Yiddish word *tsurus* means . . .?

GEOGRAPHY 280. ➤ This town in Israel was named after Theodore Herzl . . .?

ANSWERS

CURRENT
EVENTS   273. ➤ Saudi Arabia, Algeria, Mauritania.

WOMEN   274. ➤ Mama Cass Elliot.

ARTS &
CULTURE   275. ➤ Abraham Joshua Heschel.

PEOPLE   276. ➤ Marcel Marceau.

RELIGION   277. ➤ To remember, *"Zakhar."*

HISTORY   278. ➤ The Jewish Agency.

LANGUAGE 279. ➤ Trouble.

GEOGRAPHY 280. ➤ Herzliya (established in 1924).

Trivia Judaica **QUESTIONS**

CURRENT
EVENTS 281. ➤ This fundamentalist Moslem religious and political group has become a major base of terrorist activity on Israel's northern border . . .?

WOMEN 282. ➤ To which royal female figure is the Sabbath often compared . . .?

ARTS &
CULTURE 283. ➤ This Jewish actor was the youngest ever to win an Academy Award for Best Actor, receiving it when he was 30-years-old . . .?

PEOPLE 284. ➤ The founder of *The New Republic* magazine, a Pulitzer Prize winning American Jewish journalist, was the most influential pundit of his era . . .?

RELIGION 285. ➤ The Talmud dictates that this type of person takes precedence over a king . . .?

HISTORY 286. ➤ The *Palmach* organization was created before the establishment of the State of Israel. Why was it formed . . .?

LANGUAGE 287. ➤ What does the Yiddish word *goy* literally mean...?

GEOGRAPHY 288. ➤ In what country was Adolf Eichmann captured and where was he brought to trial . . .?

ANSWERS

EVENTS 281. ➤ The Followers of *Hammas,* or the "Party of God."

WOMEN 282. ➤ A queen.

ARTS &
CULTURE 283. ➤ Richard Dreyfus.

PEOPLE 284. ➤ Walter Lippmann.

RELIGION 285. ➤ The scholar.

HISTORY 286. ➤ To provide the *Haganah* with a reserve of crack soldiers—always ready for special military missions against the enemies of Israel.

LANGUAGE 287. ➤ "Nation," although it is most often used in a pejorative sense to refer to an individual who is not Jewish.

GEOGRAPHY 288. ➤ He was captured in Argentina, and brought to trial in Israel.

CURRENT
EVENTS   289. ➤ The Vatican's embassy in Israel will be
              situated in what non-Jewish enclave. . .?

WOMEN   290. ➤ Theodosia Goodman was the original name
              of this Jewish silent film star. . .?

ARTS &
CULTURE 291. ➤ This Jewish singing duo started out with
              the stage names of *Tom and Jerry*, but later
              returned to their original names, which
              were . . .?

PEOPLE   292. ➤ This English philanthropist provided the
              funds for the construction of the first com-
              mercial vineyards in Israel...?

RELIGION 293. ➤ These characteristics identify a fish that is
              kosher. . .?

HISTORY 294. ➤ Name two of the first three nations that
              formally recognized the State of Israel in
              1948. . .?

LANGUAGE 295. ➤ Israel's General Federation of Jewish La-
              bor, founded in December 1920, is called
              . . .?

GEOGRAPHY296. ➤ Which three American states have the
              largest percentages of Jewish residents
              . . .?

ANSWERS

CURRENT
EVENTS   289. ➤ **Jaffo, the heavily Arabic sister city of Tel Aviv.**

WOMEN   290. ➤ **Theda Bara.**

ARTS &
CULTURE   291. ➤ *Simon and Garfunkel.*

PEOPLE   292. ➤ **James R. Rothschild.**

RELIGION   293. ➤ **The fish must have both fins and scales.**

HISTORY   294. ➤ **The United States, the Soviet Union and Nicaragua.**

LANGUAGE   295. ➤ **The** *Histadrut.*

GEOGRAPHY   296. ➤ **New York, New Jersey, and Florida (Washingto, D.C. would be second, if it were a state).**

CURRENT
EVENTS   297. ➤ Arch anti-Semite, Louis Farrakhan, re-
               ceived a five million dollar "loan" from
               this radical government, in 1985. . .?

WOMEN   298. ➤ This Jewish columnist was born Sylvia
               Field Feldman, but is known today as . . .?

ARTS &
CULTURE   299. ➤ Yehuda Halevi was accomplished in this
               field of the arts . . .?

PEOPLE   300. ➤ This statesman was the first Israeli Am-
               bassador to the United States . . .?

RELIGION 301. ➤ State in English the first line of the *shema*,
               the Jewish confession of faith which is
               recited daily. . .?

HISTORY 302. ➤ He established a dynasty which lasted 400
               years, until the Babylonian conquest. He
               unified the southern and northern tribes,
               and made Jerusalem his capital . . .?

LANGUAGE 303. ➤ This language was developed by the
               Ashkenazim . .?

GEOGRAPHY 304. ➤ The Israeli settlement of Mei-Ami was
               formed in 1963, with donations from
               American Jews. The unique story behind
               the origin of its name is . . .?

ANSWERS

CURRENT
EVENTS 297. ➤ Libya. (He claimed that the money would be used to improve the economic status of Blacks in the U.S.).

WOMEN 298. ➤ Sylvia Porter.

ARTS &
CULTURE 299. ➤ Poetry (in Yiddish).

PEOPLE 300. ➤ Abba Eban.

RELIGION 301. ➤ "Hear O Israel the Lord is Our God, the Lord is One."

HISTORY 302. ➤ King David (his reign was 1004 BCE to 960 BCE).

LANGUAGE 303. ➤ Yiddish.

GEOGRAPHY 304. ➤ Jews from Miami, Florida donated the money to start this settlement and the Israeli government decided to Hebraize the name of the donors' hometown (it means "Waters of My Nation").

Trivia Judaica   **QUESTIONS**

CURRENT
EVENTS   305. ➤ Who balmed America's involvement in
               the Gulf War on American Jews who he
               referred to as Israel's "Amen corner"...?

WOMEN   306. ➤ This Jewish actress was born Shirley
               Schrift...?

ARTS &
CULTURE   307. ➤ Who played the role of Ari Ben-Canaan in
               Exodus, the classic movie about Israel's
               early modern history...?

PEOPLE   308. ➤ For the first ten years of her career, this
               financial columnist and author wrote a
               column whose byline did not disclose her
               sex...?

RELIGION 309. ➤ Which food is used as a dip on *Rosh
               Hashanah*, to symbolize the sweetness of
               the coming year...?

HISTORY   310. ➤ Israel was formally proclaimed a state at 4
               o'clock in the afternoon on this date...?

LANGUAGE 311. ➤ The period when modern European cul-
               ture was spread among the Jewish people
               is referred to as the *Haskalah*, which means
               ...?

GEOGRAPHY 312. ➤ The combined Jewish population of Eu-
               rope is (within ten percent accuracy)...?

ANSWERS

CURRENT
EVENTS **305.** ➤ **Syndicated columnist Patrick J. Buchanan.**

WOMEN **306.** ➤ **Shelley Winters.**

ARTS &
CULTURE **307.** ➤ **Paul Newman.**

PEOPLE **308.** ➤ **Sylvia Porter.**

REUGION **309.** ➤ **Honey.**

HISTORY **310.** ➤ **May 14, 1948.**

LANGUAGE **311.** ➤ **The Enlightenment.**

GEOGRAPHY **312.** ➤ **4.1 million.**

CURRENT
EVENT   313. ➤ How many Israelies died as a direct result of the 39 Iraqi scuds that damaged 9,000 homes during the Gulf War. . .?

WOMEN   314. ➤ This still-glamorous actress was known as "The Look" at the beginning of her movie career . . .?

ARTS &
CULTURE   315. ➤ This Jewish comedian and member of the Marx Brothers team was born Adolph Marx, but was known by the stage name . . .?

PEOPLE   316. ➤ This university professor and 1970 Nobel Prize winner in economics, wrote the most widely used textbook on economics. . .?

RELIGION   317. ➤ This Biblical Prophet attends every circumcision, to protect the Jewish infant from danger . . .?

HISTORY   318. ➤ How many times has Israel captured the Straits of Tiran from Egypt?

LANGUAGE 319. ➤ Russian Jews who attempted to leave their country but were prevented from doing so by their government, were referred to by this hybrid English word . . .?

GEOGRAPHY 320. ➤ This European Jewish community plays a key role in the diamond trade and is the most Orthodox in Europe . . .?

ANSWERS

CURRENT
EVENTS   313. ▶ One.

WOMEN   314. ▶ Lauren Bacall.

ARTS &
CULTURE   315. ▶ Harpo.

PEOPLE   316. ▶ Professor Paul Samuelson (of M.I.T.).

RELIGION   317. ▶ Elijah.

HISTORY   318. ▶ Twice: First, during the Sinai Campaign of 1956 (Israel captured the Straits which had been used by Egypt to hinder navigation since 1948.) Second, during the 1967 Six-Day War (Egypt seized the Straits with the express purpose of stopping Israel's traffic. (Israel retaliated and the Six-Day War began).

LANGUAGE   319. ▶ *Refuseniks*.

GEOGRAPHY   320. ▶ Antwerp, Belgium.

Trivia Judaica QUESTIONS

CURRENT
EVENTS 321. ➤ What aspect of the Walsh report on the Iran-Contra affair does Israel contest. . .?

WOMEN 322. ➤ Who was the Biblical woman Beruryah and what was unique about her . . .?

ARTS &
CULTURE 323. ➤ This Jewish comedian made his film debut in the movie *What's New Pussycat* . . .?

PEOPLE 324. ➤ How many Marx Brothers were there . . .?

RELIGION 325. ➤ Why is a *mezuzah* fixed to the doorpost in an observant Jewish home . . .?

HISTORY 326. ➤ Since the creation of the world, the largest and most dense concentration of Jews has been in this area . . .?

LANGUAGE 327. ➤ The song, *Bei Mir Bista Shein,* was the most financially successful Yiddish song of all time. In English it is known as...?

GEOGRAPHY 328. ➤ This continent has the largest number of Jewish inhabitants. . .?

ANSWERS

CURRENT
EVENTS   321. ➤ That Israel initiated the secret arms-to-Iran deal in what became known as the Iran-Contra affair.

WOMEN   322. ➤ She was the daughter of Rabbi Hanina ben Teradyon and the only female Talmudist of her time.

ARTS &
CULTURE   323. ➤ Woody Allen.

PEOPLE   324. ➤ Five.

RELIGION   325. ➤ Because it is prescribed by the Commandment stating: "Thou shalt write them (the Ten Commandments) upon the doorposts of thy house..."

HISTORY   326. ➤ The New York Metropolitan area.

LANGUAGE   327. ➤ *For Me You Are Beautiful.*

GEOGRAPHY   328. ➤ North America (est 6.5 million).

Trivia Judaica — QUESTIONS

CURRENT
EVENTS 329. ➤ What is the *Gadna* program that all Israeli high school students are required to enroll in . . .?

WOMEN 330. ➤ What outrageous Jewish female TV sitcom star was rated television's top draw since the mid-eighties. . .?

ARTS &
CULTURE 331. ➤ This Jewish author reportedly failed English in high school, but later wrote the bestselling novel, *Exodus* . . .?

PEOPLE 332. ➤ This Jewish athlete holds the world's record for winning the most gold medals in a single Olympics . . .?

RELIGION 333. ➤ What do Sephardic Jews call their most learned rabbis?

HISTORY 334. ➤ Which act of defiance sparked the Maccabean Revolt which *Chanukah* commemorates?

LANGUAGE 335. ➤ The difference between *kvetch* and *kvitch* is . . .?

GEOGRAPHY 336. ➤ In the 19th century, in this country, there were mass conversions of Jews to Christianity. . .?

ANSWERS

CURRENT
EVENTS 329. ➤ **The mandatory pre-military training. (It stands for *"Ghedudei Naor"* — or Youth Troops.)**

WOMEN 330. ➤ **Roseanne Barr.**

ARTS &
CULTURE 331. ➤ **Leon Uris.**

PEOPLE 332. ➤ **Mark Spitz.**

RELIGION 333. ➤ ***"Hachamin,"* or sages.**

HISTORY 334. ➤ **The refusal of the Maccabees to submit to the Greeks' demand that they publicly eat pork.**

LANGUAGE 335. ➤ **The former means "to complain", the latter "to squeal".**

GEOGRAPHY 336. ➤ **Germany (It didn't help them much as they were still sent to the gas chambers once the Nazis discovered their Jewish heritage).**

Trivia Judaica   **QUESTIONS**

CURRENT
EVENTS   337. ➤ At which death camp did "Ivan the Ter-
                rible" gain his notoriety (where survivors'
                testimony could not convincingly place
                Demjanjuk). . .?

WOMEN   338. ➤ She was the Prophetess that led the Israel-
                ites in dancing and praising God—after
                they escaped from Egypt. . . ?

ARTS &
CULTURE   339. ➤ This Jewish author originally published
                the book *The Education of Hyman Kaplan*,
                using the pen name Leonard Q. Ross. . . ?

PEOPLE   340. ➤ During the British rule of Palestine, this
                Jewish politician was the first High Com-
                missioner. . .?

RELIGION   341. ➤ Why is it customary for the groom to wear
                a *kittel* at a traditional Jewish wedding. . .?

HISTORY   342. ➤ When the Romans conquered the Land of
                Israel, they changed its name to . . .?

LANGUAGE   343. ➤ What are the common Hebrew words for
                the Jewish concepts of forbidden and per-
                mitted food. . .?

GEOGRAPHY 344. ➤ Which Arab country has a law barring
                Jews from ever entering it. . . ?

ANSWERS

CURRENT
EVENTS   337. ➤ **Treblinka.**

WOMEN   338. ➤ **Miriam (the sister of Moses).**

ARTS &
CULTURE   339. ➤ **Leo Rosten.**

PEOPLE   340. ➤ **Sir Herbert Samuel.**

RELIGION   341. ➤ **The white robe is a symbol of purity and rebirth.**

HISTORY   342. ➤ **Palestine.**

LANGUAGE 343. ➤ *Trayfeh* **and** *Kosher.*

GEOGRAPHY 344. ➤ **Saudi Arabia.**

CURRENT
EVENTS   345. ➤ Which leading Republican U.S. Senator, on the eve of the Gulf crisis, said that, "Saddam has constructive suggestions which could bring calm to the area". . .?

WOMEN   346. ➤ Born in 1867, this Jewish woman was active in social work and founded the Henry Street Settlement House. . .?

ARTS &
CULTURE   347. ➤ Which Jewish genius directed this 1984 humor film about a hopeless theatrical agent who was a total loser. . . ?

PEOPLE   348. ➤ This impresario presented artists such as Isadora Duncan, Arthur Rubinstein and Anna Pavlova. He also brought the *Bolshoi Ballet* to the U.S. . .?

RELIGION 349. ➤ This Jewish holiday stresses among other things the principle of liberty . . .?

HISTORY   350. ➤ What did Wisconsin's Senator Bob Kasten recently do to ensure that the U.N. would not be used as a tool of anti-Semitic forces, without suffering severe financial penalties. . . ?

LANGUAGE 351. ➤ The Yiddish word *umgelumpert* refers to one who is . . .?

GEOGRAPHY 352. ➤ In which country did the miracle of *Chanukah* occur. . . ?

ANSWERS

CURRENT
EVENTS   345. ➤ Bob Dole.

WOMEN   346. ➤ Lilian Wald.

ARTS &
CULTURE   347. ➤ Woody Allen, directing *Broadway Danny Rose.*

PEOPLE   348. ➤ Sol Hurok.

RELIGION   349. ➤ Passover. (It commemorates when the Jewish slaves in Egypt gained their freedom.)

HISTORY   350. ➤ He successfully introduced legislation that imposes permanent financial penalties on any U.N. agency that deprives Israel of its rights. (The offending agencies would lose the U.S. contribution of 25% of their budgets.)

LANGUAGE 351. ➤ Awkward.

GEOGRAPHY 352. ➤ In the country that is now Israel.

Trivia Judaica   **QUESTIONS**

CURRENT
EVENTS   353. ➤ Name the only two Jews who have been elected Mayor of New York City. . .?

WOMEN   354. ➤ This Jewish woman is Chairman of the Board of the Washington Post Company. . .?

ARTS &
CULTURE   355. ➤ Among his most popular books, this late Israeli soldier-statesman wrote *Diary of The Sinai Campaign, Living With The Bible, Breakthrough* and his autobiography, *The Story of My Life.*. . .?

PEOPLE   356. ➤ What portion of world Jewry perished during the Nazi Holocaust?

RELIGION   357. ➤ He founded the Jewish Reconstructionist Movement, in 1922. . . .?

HISTORY   358. ➤ Which ancient judge was a cruel and harsh ruler of the Jews for three years, until he was assassinated. . .?

LANGUAGE   359. ➤ The Yiddish equivalent of Italian ravioli are. . .?

GEOGRAPHY   360. ➤ In Jerusalem, on *Shavuos,* it is the custom for Jews to meet at this location at sunrise for the morning prayer service...?

ANSWERS

CURRENT
EVENTS   353. ➤ **Abraham Beame and Edward I. Koch.**

WOMEN   354. ➤ **Katherine Graham.**

ARTS &
CULTURE   355. ➤ **Moshe Dayan.**

PEOPLE   356. ➤ **One third of the Jewish people.**

RELIGION   357. ➤ **Dr. Morded Kaplan. (Their religious services are similiar to those of the Conservative Movement).**

HISTORY   358. ➤ **Abimelech.**

LANGUAGE 359. ➤ *Kreplach.*

GEOGRAPHY 360. ➤ **The Western Wall. (It is also known as the *Kotel*.)**

CURRENT
EVENTS   361. ➤ When the Communist *Sandinistas* seized
               power in Nicaragua, what did they do to
               Israel's Embassy . . .?

WOMEN   362. ➤ This Biblical book, named after a woman,
               is a love story . . .?

ARTS &
CULTURE   363. ➤ Born Ya' akov Moshe Maza, this former
               rabbi has become well known as a Jewish
               comedian whose trademark is his heavy
               Jewish accent . . .?

PEOPLE   364. ➤ This would-be Messiah was asked to choose
               between death and the Moslem faith and,
               to the horror of hundreds of thousands of
               his followers, he chose to don the turban
               . . .?

RELIGION 365. ➤ *Kiddush* is said on . . .?

HISTORY   366. ➤ In what month is Holocaust Remembrance
               Day. . .?

LANGUAGE 367. ➤ The Yiddish word *kibbitz* means . . .?

GEOGRAPHY368. ➤ Jesus was born a Jew in this town . . .?

ANSWERS

CURRENT
EVENTS 361. ➤ **They turned it over to the P.L.O. (They also closed all synagogues, confiscated property and valuables, and expelled the country's Jews.)**

WOMEN 362. ➤ **The Book of Ruth.**

ARTS &
CULTURE 363. ➤ **Jackie Mason.**

PEOPLE 364. ➤ **Shabatai Zvi, the False Messiah.**

RELIGION 365. ➤ **The Sabbath and holidays. (It is a prayer recited over a cup of wine.)**

HISTORY 366. ➤ **April (19th).**

LANGUAGE 367. ➤ **To offer unwanted advice, as a talkative bystander would while observing a game.**

GEOGRAPHY 368. ➤ **Bethlehem.**

CURRENT
EVENTS   369. ➤ Before the Holocaust, over three-and-a half million Jews lived in Poland. How many live there today (within 10% accuracy). . .?

WOMEN   370. ➤ This Dutch Jewish girl is known throughout the world for the writing she did while hiding from the Nazis in Amsterdam . . .?

ARTS &
CULTURE   371. ➤ This Jewish comedian and member of the Marx Brothers team was born Herbert Marx but was known by his stage name . . .?

PEOPLE   372. ➤ What did the Jewish scientist Judah Cresques, otherwise known as the "Map Jew" of medieval Spain, hypothesize before all others. . .?

RELIGION   373. ➤ According to the Story of Creation, what existed on the first day of the world?

HISTORY   374. ➤ Before World War I, Jewish financiers refused to make loans to this government . . .?

LANGUAGE 375. ➤ This traditional Jewish food is a baked or fried roll of dough, usually filled with mashed potato or meat . . .?

GEOGRAPHY376. ➤ Lake Kinneret, in Northern Israel, is commonly referred to by this name. . .?

ANSWERS

CURRENT
EVENTS 369. ➤ About 5,000 remain. (The virulent anti-Semitism of the Polish population lingered on even after the Holocaust, inspiring the remaining Jews to resettle elsewhere.)

WOMEN 370. ➤ Anne Frank.

ARTS &
CULTURE 371. ➤ Zeppo.

PEOPLE 372. ➤ That the Earth was round (200 years before Copernicus).

RELIGION 373. ➤ Light and darkness.

HISTORY 374. ➤ The Soviet Union because of the murderous Pogroms encouraged by the Russian government.

LANGUAGE 375. ➤ A Knish.

GEOGRAPHY 376. ➤ The Sea of Galilee.

Trivia Judaica   **QUESTIONS**

CURRENT
EVENTS   377. ➤ Israel has been refused membership in the
International Red Cross because . . .?

WOMEN   378. ➤ What item must an Orthodox Jewish
woman have in her possession or know the
exact whereabouts of—in order to prop-
erly live with her husband?

ARTS &
CULTURE   379. ➤ This Jewish writer won the 1976 Pulitzer
Prize for Fiction for his book, *The Fixer*. . .?

PEOPLE   380. ➤ He founded the Zionist Youth Movement,
Betar, in 1923 . . .?

RELIGION   381. ➤ Why does the pious Jew believe that he
should always cover his head as a sign of
respect for God?

HISTORY   382. ➤ Enacted by the Knesset in 1950, this law
grants automatic Israeli citizenship to Jew-
ish immigrants. . .?

LANGUAGE 383. ➤ The Yiddish expression *kochleffel*
means. . .?

GEOGRAPHY 384. ➤ This holy city in Israel was King David's
first capital . . .?

ANSWERS

377. ➤ **Official Reason: The only two symbols recognized by the Red Cross are the Cross and the Arab Crescent—the Star of David is not acceptable and since Israel uses this symbol she cannot be a member.**

Real Reason: The 21 Arab states that belong have threatened to withdraw if Israel is allowed to join.

WOMEN 378. ➤ **The "*ketubah,*" or Jewish marriage contract.**

ARTS &
CULTURE 379. ➤ **Bernard Malamud.**

PEOPLE 380. ➤ **Vladimir Ze'ev Jabotinsky.**

RELIGION 381. ➤ **Because he considers himself always standing before God.**

HISTORY 382. ➤ **The Law of Return.**

LANGUAGE 383. ➤ **One who stirs up trouble. (Literally: cooking with a spoon).**

GEOGRAPHY 384. ➤ **Hebron.**

CURRENT
EVENTS   385. ➤ What is the full name of the Gentile res-
                   cuer of Jews who was the subject of Steven
                   Spielberg's movie. . .?

WOMEN   386. ➤ This 1983 Jewish-theme film has been
                   called "the most lavish film ever to feature
                   a Jewish female leading role". . .?

ARTS &
CULTURE   387. ➤ He was born Leonard Rosenberg and was
                   the fastidious half of a popular TV situa-
                   tion comedy adapted from a successful
                   movie . . .?

PEOPLE   388. ➤ This Jewish entrepreneur invented the
                   Polaroid camera . . .?

RELIGION   389. ➤ What are the *aidim* at traditional Jewish
                   marriage ceremonies supposed to wit-
                   ness. . .?

HISTORY   390. ➤ How was Israeli super-spy Eli Cohen dis-
                   covered by the Syrians. . .?

LANGUAGE 391. ➤ The Russian word for "devastation" is a
                   derivative of this term that unfortunately
                   describes what frequently happened to
                   Russian Jews during and prior to WW I
                   and WW II . . .?

GEOGRAPHY 392. ➤ It is alleged that this African country has
                   assisted Israel's development of nuclear
                   weapons. . .?

ANSWERS

CURRENT
EVENTS 385. ➤ Oskar Schindler.

WOMEN 386. ➤ *"Yentl"* (directed by and starring Barbra Streisand).

ARTS &
CULTURE 387. ➤ Tony Randall (as Felix Unger in *The Odd Couple*).

PEOPLE 388. ➤ Edward Land.

RELIGION 389. ➤ The signing of the *"ketuba"* or marriage contract.

HISTORY 390. ➤ The Soviet Union had provided Syria with advanced electronic surveillance equipment that uncovered Cohen's secret radio transmissions to Israel.

LANGUAGE 391. ➤ "Pogroms." (The organized devastation of Jewish life and property by anti-semites.)

GEOGRAPHY 392. ➤ South Africa.

CURRENT
EVENTS   393. ➤ Has Jordan's King Hussein. picked his oldest or youngest son, to be his heir. . .?

WOMEN   394. ➤ Which aspect of the deity is always expressed in the feminine. . .?

ARTS &
CULTURE   395. ➤ Yigael Yadin, Israel's second Chief of Staff, later became a leading Israeli scientist in this field and made several major discoveries . . .?

PEOPLE   396. ➤ What famous Jewish baseball player, the youngest (26) ever elected to the Hall of Fame, refused to play on Rosh Hashana and Yom Kippur?

RELIGION   397. ➤ The Day of Judgement refers to this day—known by a more popular name. . .?

HISTORY   398. ➤ The 1956 Egyptian-Israeli War is more commonly referred to as . . .?

LANGUAGE 399. ➤ The Yiddish word *haimish* literally means. . .?

GEOGRAPHY400. ➤ This Biblical place was described in the book of Zechariah as the "City of Peace and Truth". . .?

ANSWERS

CURRENT
EVENTS 392. ➤ Neither. The Crown Prince is his younger brother.

WOMEN 393. ➤ The *Shechinah*, or Divine Presence.

ARTS &
CULTURE 395. ➤ Archaelogy (he explored Hazor and Masada).

PEOPLE 396. ➤ Sandy Koufax.

RELIGION 397. ➤ Yom Kippur or the Day of Atonement.

HISTORY 398. ➤ The Sinai Campaign.

LANGUAGE 399. ➤ Friendly and down-to-earth.

GEOGRAPHY 400. ➤ Jerusalem.

CURRENT
EVENTS 401. ➤ In 1985, the United States Supreme Court decided to hear a case dealing with whether an observant Jew could wear this kind of forbidden religious garb while serving in the armed forces . . .?

WOMEN 402. ➤ The *Bat Mitzvah* ceremony for Jewish females originated within this Jewish movement . . .?

ARTS &
CULTURE 403. ➤ This renowned Jewish astronomer won a Pulitzer Prize in 1978 for his book *The Dragons of Eden* . . .?

PEOPLE 404. ➤ This Israeli spy working in Damascus managed to become the top aide to the Syrian defense minister, before he was uncovered and executed in 1965. . .?

RELIGION 405. ➤ What does *maror* symbolize at the Passover Seder. . .?

HISTORY 406. ➤ This late Egyptian leader repeatedly referred to the anti-Semitic tome *The Protocols of the Elders of Zion* to document his charge that three hundred Zionists ruled the world. . .?

LANGUAGE 407. ➤ This garment is called *gatkes*. . .?

GEOGRAPHY408. ➤ The first Jewish astronaut was a citizen of this country. . .?

ANSWERS

CURRENT
EVENTS   401. ➤ **A yarmulke.**

WOMEN   402. ➤ **The Reconstructionist (in 1922).**

ARTS &
CULTURE   403. ➤ **Dr. Carl Sagan.**

PEOPLE   404. ➤ **Eli Cohen.**

RELIGION   405. ➤ **This bitter herb represents the bitter life of the Jewish slaves.**

HISTORY   406. ➤ **Gamel Abdul Nasser.**

LANGUAGE 407. ➤ **Long johns.**

GEOGRAPHY 408. ➤ **The U.S.S.R. (Boris Volynov).**

Trivia Judaica   **QUESTIONS**

CURRENT
EVENTS   409. ➤ Israel's large and successful Intel corpora-
tion manufactures what kinds of prod-
ucts. . .?

WOMEN   410. ➤ Who was the Jewish astronaut killed in the
Challenger space shuttle disaster. . .?

ARTS &
CULTURE   411. ➤ This Jewish comedian said, "I don't want
to belong to any club that accepts people
like me as members." . . .?

PEOPLE   412. ➤ This celebrated songwriter wrote a song
for pop-star Madonna which won an Os-
car. Name him. . .?

RELIGION 413. ➤ The longest book of the *Torah* is . . .?

HISTORY   414. ➤ One of the first acts of Iran's Ayatollah
Khomeini after he assumed power was the
takeover of . . .?

LANGUAGE 415. ➤ What is the meaning of the Hebrew greet-
ing *Shavua Tov*, used after the conclusion
of the Sabbath?

GEOGRAPHY 416. ➤ This European nation has the largest number of Jewish citizens . . .?

ANSWERS

CURRENT
EVENTS   **409.** ➤ **Computer chips and high tech related products.**

WOMEN   **410.** ➤ **Judith Reznick**

ARTS &
CULTURE   **411.** ➤ **Groucho Marx.**

PEOPLE   **412.** ➤ **Stephen Sondheim. (The song was *Sooner or Later* from the movie *Dick Tracy*.)**

RELIGION   **413.** ➤ **Genesis.**

HISTORY   **414.** ➤ **The Israeli Embassy in Tehran.**

LANGUAGE   **415.** ➤ **"Have a good week."**

GEOGRAPHY   **416.** ➤ **France (est. 700,000).**

CURRENT
EVENTS   417. ➤ The Israeli government referred to the
               1982 war in Lebanon by this alternative
               English name . . .?

WOMEN   418. ➤ This 1967 movie, starring a Jewish fe-
               male, signaled a new pride in being Jew-
               ish. The star was playing up her heritage
               instead of avoiding it . . .?

ARTS &
CULTURE   419. ➤ He was the most famous Jewish actor in
               The Wizard of Oz. playing the role of a not-
               so-wild animal . . .?

PEOPLE   420. ➤ This Jewish hero lost his life while defend-
               ing the northern settlement of Tel Hai
               against Arab attackers in 1920. His im-
               mortal last words were "No matter; it is
               good to die for our country". . .?

RELIGION 421. ➤ On which holiday is it customary in some
               Jewish homes to serve a cooked fish-head
               with the meal . . .?

HISTORY   422. ➤ He was the President of the United States
               when America recognized the new State of
               Israel. . .?

LANGUAGE 423. ➤ The much overused Yiddish expression,
               maven, refers to . . .?

GEOGRAPHY 424. ➤ In 1972, world attention focused on 31
               Connallystrasse Street in Munich because
               of this notorious event. . .?

ANSWERS

CURRENT
EVENTS   417. ➤ **"Operation Peace for Galilee".**

WOMEN   418. ➤ ***"Funny Girl,"*** **starring Barbra Streisand. She played the Jewish Fanny Brice.**

ARTS &
CULTURE   419. ➤ **Bert Lahr (the Cowardly Lion).**

PEOPLE   420. ➤ **Joseph Trumpeldor.**

RELIGION   421. ➤ **Rosh Hashanah (it symbolically represents the 'head' of the year).**

HISTORY   422. ➤ **Harry S. Truman.**

LANGUAGE 423. ➤ **An expert (it comes form the Hebrew "he who understands").**

GEOGRAPHY 424. ➤ **It was the living quarters of the Israeli athletes at the Olympic Village, who were taken hostage and murdered by PLO terrorists.**

CURRENT
EVENTS   425. ➤ How was the contoversy over the Carmelite
               Convent on the grounds of Auschwitz
               resolved. . .?

WOMEN   426. ➤ Israel's first ever olympic medal was won
               by a woman sabra competing in what
               sport. . .?

ARTS &
CULTURE   427. ➤ This Australian writer won Britain's pres-
               tigious Booker Literary Prize for his book
               Schindler's List which was about Oskar
               Schindler's rescue of over 900 Jews during
               World War II . . .?

PEOPLE   428. ➤ This popular Jewish leader and rabbi, from
               Riverdale New York, is at the forefront of
               the campaign to right the unjust and dis-
               proportionate jail sentence received by
               Jonathan Pollard. . . ?

RELIGION 429. ➤ What is another name for the eighth day of
               Tabernacles?

HISTORY   430. ➤ This former army paratrooper was the first
               Israeli-born Ambassador to the United
               Nations . . .?

LANGUAGE 431. ➤ One who thinks like a smart Jewish person
               is often referred to in Yiddish as one with
               a . . .?

GEOGRAPHY 432. ➤ Moses Maimonides was the personal phy-
               sician to the royal family of this coun-
               try. . .?

ANSWERS

CURRENT
EVENTS 425. ➤ The nuns finally relocated nearby, but
off the camp grounds. (Only after years
of major political pressure was brought
upon them by Jewish leaders who were
horrified that this landmark to remind
the world of Jewish destruction was being encroached upon by a local Christian religious group).

WOMEN 426. ➤ Judo.

ARTS &
CULTURE 427. ➤ Thomas Keneally (who is not Jewish).

PEOPLE 428. ➤ Rabbi Avi Weiss.

RELIGION 429. ➤ *"Sh'mini Atzereth"* or the Eighth Day of
Assembly. (It marks the dose of the
festival.)

HISTORY 430. ➤ Benjamin Netanyahu.

LANGUAGE 431. ➤ *"Yiddishe kop."*(Jewish head.)

GEOGRAPHY 432. ➤ Egypt.

Trivia Judaica QUESTIONS

CURRENT
EVENTS   433. ➤ Why do many charge that Jonathan Pollard was punished much too severely. . .?

WOMEN   434. ➤ She is the Jewish half of a popular morning
talk show, always talking and joking about
her child and famous former football player
husband. . .?

ARTS &
CULTURE   435. ➤ What was unique about the boxing shorts
worn by Jewish boxer Max Baer?

PEOPLE   436. ➤ He was known as the "Prophet of the State
of Israel" . . .?

RELIGION 437. ➤ In this Book of the Bible, the concept of
monotheism is central and emphasized
repeatedly. . .?

HISTORY   438. ➤ In this European country, synagogues and
Jewish cultural organizations are never
considered as tax-exempt institutions, rabbis are not excused from military service
and the rabbinate, when offering legal
testimony, enjoys no rights of confidenti-
ality in matters relating to the Jewish
ministry . . .?

LANGUAGE 439. ➤ He is considered the father of modern
Hebrew. . .?

GEOGRAPHY 440. ➤ What was significant in Jewish history
about Pernambuco, Brazil, in 1654. . .?

ANSWERS

CURRENT
EVENTS 433. ➤ He got a much harsher penalty than those spying for America's enemies. (He also was promised a plea bargain by the prosecution—as an inducement to plead guilty—which was inexplicably not honored by the U.S Government).

WOMEN 434. ➤ Kathy Lee Gifford (from *Regis and Kathy Lee*).

ARTS &
CULTURE 435. ➤ He had a Star of David sewn on them.

PEOPLE 436. ➤ Theodor Herzl.

RELIGION 437. ➤ Deuteronomy.

HISTORY 438. ➤ Spain. (A new set of laws to grant rabbis the same privileges enjoyed by priests is under review.)

LANGUAGE 439. ➤ Eliezer Ben Yehuda.

GEOGRAPHY 440. ➤ The first Jewish group that arrived in North America departed from this city.

Trivia Judaica   QUESTIONS

CURRENT
EVENTS   441. ➤ Which three Arab countries have allowed Israeli delegates to attend their international forums. . .?

WOMEN   442. ➤ Golda Meir's first political post in the State of Israel was . . .?

ARTS &
CULTURE   443. ➤ Amos Oz, A.B. Yehoshua, Amos Elon and Yehuda Amichai all share this distinction. . .?

PEOPLE   444. ➤ This Jewish jurist was appointed to the Supreme Court in 1965, and resigned in 1969. . .?

RELIGION   445. ➤ Why is *Yom Kippur* eve the only time Jews wear *talit* in the evening?

HISTORY   446. ➤ In 1825, Mordecai Manuel Noah attempted to establish a homeland for European Jews to be called Ararat—in this part of the United States . . .?

LANGUAGE 447. ➤ This commonly used English term was coined in 1879 by Wilhelm Marr, a notorious despiser of Jews, as a euphemistic substitute for "Jew-hater" . . .?

GEOGRAPHY448. ➤ These Biblical rivers, Pishon, Tigni, Givon and Euphrates—all flowed in the general vicinity of this well-known Biblical location. . .?

ANSWERS

CURRENT
EVENTS 441. ➤ **Morocco, Egypt and Tunisia.**

WOMEN 442. ➤ **Israel's Ambassador to the Soviet Union.**

ARTS &
CULTURE 443. ➤ **They are widely acclaimed and widely translated Israeli writers.**

PEOPLE 444. ➤ **The Honorable Abe Fortas.**

RELIGION 445. ➤ **Because all of "Yom Kippur" is considered to be part of one day. Thus, the "talit", which can only be worn during daylight hours, is appropriate.**

HISTORY 446. ➤ **In New York State. (He proposed that the settlement be on Grant Island off the Niagara River. The U.S. government refused the proposal.)**

LANGUAGE 447. ➤ **Anti-Semitism.**

GEOGRAPHY 448. ➤ **The Garden of Eden.**

Trivia Judaica   **QUESTIONS**

CURRENT
EVENTS   449. ➤ The World Trade Center bombings and related crimes were all hatched in a modest mosque located where. . .?

WOMEN   450. ➤ This leading Jewish feminist leader was born Betty Naomi Goldstein . . .?

ARTS &
CULTURE   451. ➤ The Jewish creator of Paramount Pictures, Adolph Zukor, founded another type of entertainment that is still widely popular but now costs about twenty-five times more than it did originally. . .?

PEOPLE   452. ➤ This assimilated Jewish psychiatrist and social critic began working with Theodor Herzl in 1895 and went on to become a co-founder of the World Zionist Organization. . .?

RELIGION   453. ➤ The Shabbat between Rosh Hashanah and Yom Kippur is called. . .?

HISTORY   454. ➤ For what political achievement is Zalman Shazar most noted?

LANGUAGE 455. ➤ The abbreviation for the Jewish "Organization for Vocational Training" is . . .?

GEOGRAPHY 456. ➤ In which part of the world did most of the Jewish schools known as *Cheders* operate. . .?

ANSWERS

CURRENT
EVENTS 449. ➤ In Jersey City, New Jersey.

WOMEN 450. ➤ Betty Friedan.

ARTS &
CULTURE 451. ➤ The Penny Arcade.

PEOPLE 452. ➤ Dr. Max Nordau.

RELIGION 453. ➤ *"Shabbat Shuva."* (The Sabbath of return.)

HISTORY 454. ➤ He served as President of the State of Israel (from 1963 to 1973).

LANGUAGE 455. ➤ O.R.T.

GEOGRAPHY 456. ➤ Eastern Europe.

Trivia Judaica   QUESTIONS

CURRENT
EVENTS   457. ➤ Statistically speaking, who are the most likely murder victims in Israel's disputed territories. . .?

WOMEN   458. ➤ Jacob had twelve sons and one daughter. What was her name. . . ?

ARTS &
CULTURE   459. ➤ In his autobiography, *For the Life of Me*, this noted Irish Jew, who was also a Mayor in Ireland, wrote about how he helped teach guerrilla warfare tactics to members of the Palestine Jewish underground group, the *Irgun Zvie Leumi*. . .?

PEOPLE   460. ➤ This mass-murderer was in charge of implementing Hitler's "Final Solution". . .?

RELIGION   461. ➤ According to Jewish law, which is preferable to use in a *Chanukah* menorah— candles or oil?

HISTORY   462. ➤ These two nations had the largest Jewish communities during Medieval times. . .?

LANGUAGE 463. ➤ This Jewish word means both righteousness and charity . . .?

GEOGRAPHY 464. ➤ Which contemporary Arab Capitols were once part of ancient Israel. . . ?

ANSWERS

CURRENT
EVENTS **457.** ➤ **Arabs. (The various terrorist organizations who control the territories regularly murder fellow Arabs accused of collaborating with Israel.)**

WOMEN **458.** ➤ **Dinah.**

ARTS
CULTURE **459.** ➤ **Robert Briscoe (the former mayor of Dublin, Ireland).**

PEOPLE **460.** ➤ **Adolph Eichmann.**

RELIGION **461.** ➤ **Oil (especially olive oil).**

HISTORY **462.** ➤ **Spain and Germany.**

LANGUAGE **463.** ➤ *"Tzedakah."*

GEOGRAPHY **464.** ➤ **Damascus and Amman.**

Trivia Judaica   QUESTIONS

CURRENT
EVENTS   465. ➤ Name the blind Moslem cleric said to be behind the World Trade Center bombing and other terrorist acts in the U.S. and Egypt. . .?

WOMEN   466. ➤ She founded the Women's Zionist Organization, *Hadassah* . . .?

ARTS &
CULTURE   467. ➤ These Jewish actors were known as the "Royal Family" of the Yiddish theater and their surname was . . .?

PEOPLE   468. ➤ This noted Jewish scientist gave the first official lecture at the Hebrew University of Jerusalem . . .?

RELIGION   469. ➤ What is the position of the right-wing Orthodox rabbinate on the recognition of Conservative and Reform rabbis as authentic rabbis . . .?

HISTORY   470. ➤ Daniel Webster dedicated the Bunker Hill monument in Charlestown, Massachusetts, and referred to this "Christian and Jew" who made the memorial possible. . .?

LANGUAGE   471. ➤ The Hebrew word *nasi* refers to?

GEOGRAPHY 472. ➤ The direction from Jerusalem to Tel Aviv is. . .?

ANSWERS

CURRENT
EVENTS 465. ➤ **Sheik Omar Abdel-Rahman. (In addition, he is also being charged with murdering an Egyptian-American residing in the U.S. in the early 1990's)**

WOMEN 466. ➤ **Henrietta Szold.**

ARTS &
CULTURE 467. ➤ **Adler (Stella, Celia, Luther and Jacob).**

PEOPLE 468. ➤ **Albert Einstein, in 1928.**

RELIGION 469. ➤ **They do not recognize non-Orthodox rabbis as valid rabbis. (They view them in a similar light to "witch doctors").**

HISTORY 470. ➤ **Judah Tuoro was the Jewish philanthropist and Amos Lawrence the Christian benefactor (in 1843).**

LANGUAGE 471. ➤ **President.**

GEOGRAPHY 472. ➤ **West.**

CURRENT
EVENTS   473. ➤ How many Israeli aircraft were shot down by the Syrians during "Operation Peace for Galilee. . .?"

WOMEN   474. ➤ After Eleazer and Phineas died, which woman ruled the holy city of Shiloh?

ARTS &
CULTURE   475. ➤ This Jewish actor played the role of Nazi "Colonel Klink" on the TV series *Hogan's Heroes . . .?*

PEOPLE   476. ➤ ABC-TV and NBC-TV both have Jewish anchors on their national morning news shows: ABC's *Good Morning America* and *CBS This Morning*. Name them. . .?

RELIGION   477. ➤ The founder of the American Conservative Jewish movement is . . .?

HISTORY   478. ➤ Arthur Goldberg resigned this position when President Lyndon B. Johnson asked him to accept the appointment as U.S. Ambassador to the UN . . .?

LANGUAGE 479. ➤ When does one say *L'chayim?*

GEOGRAPHY 480. ➤ The Maccabees were born in . . .?

ANSWERS

CURRENT
EVENTS 473. ➤ None. (Over 100 Arab fighter planes were shot down. Israel lost one helicopter due to technical difficulties, not because of enemy fire.)

WOMEN 474. ➤ Deborah (the great Judge).

ARTS &
CULTURE 475. ➤ Werner Klemperer.

PEOPLE 476. ➤ Joan Lunden on ABC's *Good Morning America* and Paula Zahn on *CBS This Morning*--she's Jewish by marriage. (She could be called Paula Zahn-Cohen).

RELIGION 477. ➤ Solomon Schechter (in 1902).

HISTORY 478. ➤ Associate Justice of the United States Supeme Court.

LANGUAGE 479. ➤ When taking a drink, usually alcohol.

GEOGRAPHY480. ➤ Modiin.

CURRENT
EVENTS   481. ➤ Yitzak Shamir was replaced as head of the *Likud* party by whom. . .?

WOMEN   482. ➤ The biblical Yael slew the enemy General Sisera after plying him with what beverage. . .?

ARTS &
CULTURE   483. ➤ This Jewish author wrote these recent bestselling Jewish theme novels, *The Book of Rachel* and *The Lives of Rachel*. . .?

PEOPLE   484. ➤ The leader of this terrorist group conspired to kidnap President Nixon and secretary of State Henry Kissinger, blow up the FBI's headquarters in New York, and to blow up NYC tunnels. What is his name. . .?

RELIGION   485. ➤ When asked to define the essence of Jewish law, he replied, "What is hateful to yourself, do not do to your neighbor" . . .?

HISTORY   486. ➤ In 1936, this Socialist leader became the first Jewish premier of France; four years later, he was a prisoner in a Nazi concentration camp . . .?

LANGUAGE 487. ➤ One who is *ferblondget* is . . .?

GEOGRAPHY 488. ➤ On the shores of Israel's Red Sea is an industry that cuts, polishes, and exports rock of this type. . .?

ANSWERS

CURRENT
EVENTS   481. ➤ **Benjamin Netanyahu.**

WOMEN   482. ➤ **Milk.**

ARTS &
CULTURE   483. ➤ **Joel Gross.**

PEOPLE   484. ➤ **Sheik Omar Abdel-Rahman.**

RELIGION   485. ➤ **Hillel.**

HISTORY   486. ➤ **Leon Blum.**

LANGUAGE 487. ➤ **Hopelessly lost.**

GEOGRAPHY488. ➤ **Granite.**

CURRENT
EVENTS   489. ➤ Athletes from this country were not permitted to take part in Israel's 12th
Maccabiah Games, so some disguised
themselves as new immigrants in order to
participate. . .?

WOMEN   490. ➤ Jordan's King Hussein secretly met with
this woman in late September of 1973 to
inform her of Syrian and Egyptian inten-
tions to invade Israel. . .?

ARTS &
CULTURE 491. ➤ This Jewish TV actor has won seven Emmy
awards—more than any other actor. Name
him. . .?

PEOPLE   492. ➤ This Jewish comedian was temporarily
taken off the air when he asked his "Kiddy
Viewers" to look in their parents' hand-
bags and send him some of "that green
stuff". . .?

RELIGION 493. ➤ When are the Ten Days of Repententance?

HISTORY 494. ➤ Who were the misguided and cowardly
Donmeh Jews of Turkey?

LANGUAGE 495. ➤ The Hebrew word *nefesh* translates to . . .?

GEOGRAPHY 496. ➤ Where was King Solomon's navy located. . .?

ANSWERS

CURRENT
EVENTS   489. ➤South Africa. (An international Olympic forum required Israel not to accept South Africa's Jewish athletes).

WOMEN   490. ➤ Golda Meir.

ARTS &
CULTURE 491. ➤ Ed Asner.

PEOPLE   492. ➤ Soupy Sales (Milton Hines).

RELIGION 493. ➤ Between *"Rosh Hashanah"* and *"Yom Kippur."*

HISTORY   494. ➤ The Turkish Jews who became Moslems with the false Messiah, "Shabbatai Zvi." (The Turkish authorities ordered them to renounce their Jewish religion and they complied rather than face death.)

LANGUAGE 495. ➤ Soul.

GEOGRAPHY496. ➤ On the shores of the Red Sea, in Ezion Geber (Source: Kings).

Trivia Judaica **QUESTIONS**

CURRENT
EVENTS 497. ➤ Which U.S. government official recommended a life sentence and no parole for Jonathan Pollard. . .?

WOMEN 498. ➤ In 1985, Amy Eilberg achieved distinction in the Conservative movement for this reason . . .?

ARTS &
CULTURE 499. ➤ This carrot dish is traditionally served on *Rosh Hashanah* . . .?

PEOPLE 500. ➤ This recipient of the 1976 Nobel Prize for Literature wrote a critically acclaimed personal account of his visit to Israel. Who is he and what is the title of the book?

RELIGION 501. ➤ According to the Bible, what did God create on the 7th day. . .?

HISTORY 502. ➤ The Jewish settlers in Palestine faced this ironic dilemma in their decision to join the British in fighting the Nazis. . .?

LANGUAGE 503. ➤ The Yiddish term *Geshrei* means . . .?

GEOGRAPHY504. ➤ Until recently, this European nation did not fully recognize Judaism, so marriages had to be conducted by both religious and civil authorities to be legally accepted. . .?

ANSWERS

497. ➤ Former Secretary of Defense, Caspar Weinberger. (This was contrary to the plea bargain arrangement negotiated between the prosecution and Pollard's attorneys. Weinberger was the main reason the plea bargain deal was broken by the judge presiding over the case, dooming Pollard to life in prison, unless a presidential pardon sets him free in consideration of the eight years he has already served).

WOMEN 498. ➤ She became their first female rabbi.

ARTS &
CULTLURE 499. ➤ *Tzimmes.*

PEOPLE 500. ➤ Saul Bellow, author of *"To Jerusalem and Back."*

RELIGION 501. ➤ Nothing. It was the sabbath--a time to rest.

HISTORY 502. ➤ The Jews of Palestine were fighting against the British for greater rights and freedoms at the same time that they agreed to help the British fight the Nazis.

LANGUAGE 503. ➤ To yell or to scream.

GEOGRAPHY 504. ➤ Spain.

CURRENT
EVENTS   505. ➤ Who was the young Hassidic scholar re-
               cently killed by a mob of Black youths in
               New York. . .?

WOMEN   506. ➤ In what business does Steven Speilberg's
               mother keep herself busy in L.A.. . .?

ARTS &
CULTURE   507. ➤ He wrote *A Jew In Love, Perfidy, The
               Sensualist, Child Of The Century*, and
               other outstanding 20th Century American
               literature. . .?

PEOPLE   508. ➤ He was the first English Jew to join the
               House of Lords. . .?

RELIGION 509. ➤ He was the founder of the Jewish
               Reconstructionist Movement of the United
               States . . .?

HISTORY   510. ➤ He originally built the city of Caesarea. . .?

LANGUAGE 511. ➤ What is a *blech* . . .?

GEOGRAPHY 512. ➤ When Blacks recently took power in this
               small African nation, replacing the previ-
               ous White minority government, nearly
               their entire Jewish community fled. What
               was the country's name then and now. . .?

ANSWERS

CURRENT
EVENTS 505. ➤ **Yankel Rosenbaum.**

WOMEN 506. ➤ **She runs a Kosher Delicatessen.**

ARTS &
CULTLIRE 507. ➤ **Ben Hecht.**

PEOPLE 508. ➤ **Nathaniel Rothschild.**

RELIGION 509. ➤ **Mordecai Kaplan.**

HISTORY 510. ➤ **Herod The Great.**

LANGUAGE 511 ➤ **A hot plate left on the stove for the duration of the Sabbath, in order to keep food warm without cooking,**

GEOGRAPHY512 ➤ **Rhodesia, now called Zimbabwe.**

CURRENT
EVENTS   513. ➤ What has been the Reform movement's
               most controversial action since accepting
               Jews of patrilineal descent. . .?

WOMEN   514. ➤ She is the most popular female sex-thera-
               pist in America, appearing regularly on
               TV and radio talk shows. . .?

ARTS &
CULTURE 515. ➤ This comic played one of Dick Van Dyke's
               foils on the *"Dick Van Dyke Show"* and
               was a co-writer of the Andrews Sisters'
               World War II smash *"Rum and Coca-
               Cola."* Name him. . .?

PEOPLE   516. ➤ She played Lily Von Schtupp in Mel
               Brooks' *Blazing Saddles*. . .?

RELIGION 517. ➤ In which of the Torah's first five books is
               Moses not mentioned?

HISTORY   518. ➤ What 2 major positions did David Ben
               Gurion hold simultaneously in the early
               government of Israel?

LANGUAGE 519. ➤ One who is a *balabusta* refers to . . .?

GEOGRAPHY 520. ➤ The Bible mentions the Sea of the Philis-
               tines which today is now known as this
               ocean . . .?

ANSWERS

CURRENT
EVENTS   513. ➤ **Their announced outreach program to recruit unaffiliated gentiles to become Jews .**

WOMEN   514. ➤ **Dr. Ruth Westheimer.**

ARTS &
CULTURE   515. ➤ **Morey Amsterdam.**

PEOPLE   516. ➤ **Madeline Kahn.**

RELIGION   517. ➤ **In Genesis (the first book).**

HISTORY   518. ➤ **Defense Minister and Prime Minister.**

LANGUAGE 519. ➤ **An excellent and hospitable home maker.**

GEOGRAPHY 520. ➤ **The Mediterranean.**

Trivia Judaica   **QUESTIONS**

CURRENT
EVENTS 521. ➤ While several thousand Etheopian Jews
were stranded in the Sudan, a secret letter
was drafted by the U.S. Senate and sent to
President Reagan requesting that he inter-
vene and assist these refugees get to Israel.
How many Senators signed the letter. . . ?

WOMEN 522. ➤ This Jewish singer-actress played Fanny
Brice in the movies *Funny Girl* and *Funny
Lady*. . .?

ARTS &
CULTURE 523. ➤ This Jewish songwriter composed the
monumental hit *Somewhere Over the Rain-
bow* immortalized by Judy Garland. . .?

PEOPLE 524. ➤ This Jewish physicist was responsible for
the discovery of electromagnetic waves. . .
?

RELIGION 525. ➤ On Yom Kippur, according to Orthodox
Jewish Law, which type of shoes are traditionally prohibited from being worn?

HISTORY 526. ➤ Joseph Trumpeldor helped found the Jewish Legion of the British Army—but the
Legion was preceded by another military
organization, called. . . ?

LANGUAGE 527. ➤ What is the English translation for *Sefer
Torah*?

GEOGRAPHY 528. ➤ Between World War I and World War II,
this continent had the largest Jewish population. . .?

ANSWERS

CURRENT
EVENTS **521.** ➤ **The entire U.S. Senate. (There were actually 106 signatures—six Senators accidentally signed twice!)**

WOMEN **522.** ➤ **Barbra Streisand.**

ARTS &
CULTURE **523.** ➤ **Howard Arlen.**

PEOPLE **524.** ➤ **Heinrich R. Hertz.**

RELIGION **525.** ➤ **Leather shoes. (When one is praying on the subject of life, it would be callous to wear leather which represents the death of an animal.)**

HISTORY **526.** ➤ **The Zion Mule Corps.**

LANGUAGE **527.** ➤ **Scroll of the Law.**

GEOGRAPHY **528.** ➤ **Europe.**

CURRENT
EVENTS   529. ➤ Name the two camps outside of Beirut, where Christian militia men massacred Palestinian refugees. . .?

WOMEN   530. ➤ How did God punish Miriam for speaking against Moses. . .?

ARTS &
CULTURE   531. ➤ His comedy albums of the early 60's included "*My Son, The Nut*" and "*My Son The Folksinger*." What is his name. . .?

PEOPLE   532. ➤ Who was Bogdan Chmielnicki and what were his crimes?

RELIGION   533. ➤ Who was the first Jew to be circumcised at the age of eight days?

HISTORY   534. ➤ How did the "Black Death" plague, in 14th Century Europe, affect the Jewish people?

LANGUAGE   535. ➤ The much overused Yiddish expression *knocker* means . . .?

GEOGRAPHY   536. ➤ What country is directly east of Israel. . .?

ANSWERS

CURRENT
EVENTS 529. ➤ **Sabra and Shatila.**

WOMEN 530. ➤ **With Leprosy.**

ARTS &
CULTURE 531. ➤ **Allan Sherman.**

PEOPLE 532. ➤ **A Polish hero who was the Cossack leader responsible for killing hundreds of thousands of Jews (most perished from 1648 to 1649).**

RELIGION 533. ➤ **Isaac, son of Abraham.**

HISTORY 534. ➤ **They were considered the cause of it and as a result became the victims of numerous pogroms. (Jews did not suffer as badly as the rest of the population from this plague because of their kosher eating habits and their general isolation from the contaminated Christian community.)**

LANGUAGE 535 ➤ **A big shot or an old-timer.**

GEOGRAPHY 536. ➤ **Jordan.**

Trivia Judaica   **QUESTIONS**

CURRENT
EVENTS   537. ➤ Israel holds the world record for having the highest percentage of its citizens employed by it's government. Within 5 % accuracy, what is this percentage?

WOMEN   538. ➤ This well-known Jewish French stage actress was an illegitimate child, had a wooden leg, and was fond of sleeping in a coffin . . .?

ARTS &
CULTURE   539. ➤ This Jewish actor played Harry Houdini in the 1953 movie *Houdini*. Also, what was Houdini's real name. . .?

PEOPLE   540. ➤ This Israeli statesman was born with the name Aubrey Solomon, but is better known by this name . . .?

RELIGION   541. ➤ This Book of the Bible is a series of farewell speeches by Moses, and it ends with a description of his death . . .?

HISTORY   542. ➤ What was the significant difference between the resettlement movement in Palestine, in the early 1900s, and the movement during World War II known as *Aliyah Bet*?

LANGUAGE   543. ➤ The Hebrew word *Seder* actually means . . .?

GEOGRAPHY 544. ➤ This European country was so fierce in its persecution of Jews that in 1893 the Jewish population formed an organization for its own self-defense . . .?

ANSWERS

CURRENT
EVENTS 537. ➤ **Approximately 35%. (Among the highest in the non-communist world.)**

WOMEN 538. ➤ **Sarah Bernhardt.**

ARTS &
CULTURE 539. ➤ **Tony Curtis (who was born Bernard Schwartz, played Harry Houdini—who was born Eric Weiss).**

PEOPLE 540. ➤ **Abba Eban.**

RELIGION 541. ➤ **Deuteronomy.**

HISTORY 542. ➤ **The early movement was legal and sanctioned by Turkey and Britain. *"Aliyah Bet"* was illegal and involved the smuggling of Holocaust survivors out of Europe.**

LANGUAGE 543. ➤ **Order of service.**

GEOGRAPHY 544. ➤ **Germany.**

Trivia Judaica **QUESTIONS**

CURRENT
EVENTS 545. ➤ Presently, the largest arms supplier to Saudi Arabia is . . .?

WOMEN 546. ➤ This Swiss-born Jewish female became Vermont's first woman governor. . .?

ARTS &
CULTURE 547. ➤ This old-time Jewish comedian and T.V. personality was born Joseph Abraham Gottlieb, but he used the stage name . . .?

PEOPLE 548. ➤ Jewish entrepreneur Julius Rosenwald, built this company into America's largest retailer and mail order business. . .?

RELIGION 549. ➤ In Israel, *surganiot*, or doughnuts filled with jam, are associated with which holiday. . .?

HISTORY 550. ➤ Although England is a democratic nation, what position in the British Empire is strictly off limits to all Jews forever. . .?

LANGUAGE 551. ➤ What is *Chanakah gelt* and who is it given to. . .?

GEOGRAPHY 552. ➤ The Gulf of Eilat is the meeting place of the land of which three Middle East nations. . .?

ANSWERS

CURRENT
EVENTS 545. ➤ **The United States of America.**

WOMEN 546. ➤ **Madeline Kunin (in 1985).**

ARTS &
CULTURE 547. ➤ **Joey Bishop.**

PEOPLE 548. ➤ **Sears Roebuck.**

RELIGION 549. ➤ **Chanukah (because they are fried in oil).**

HISTORY 550. ➤ **The position of Monarch. (There has been no serious Jewish protest over this restriction!)**

LANGUAGE 551. ➤ **Small gifts of money given to children as Chanukah presents.**

GEOGRAPHY 552. ➤ **Israel, Jordan and Saudi Arabia.**

Trivia Judaica   **QUESTIONS**

CURRENT
EVENTS   553. ➤ How many official languages does Israel
              have and what are they. . .?

WOMEN   554. ➤ This Biblical matriarch was not laid to rest
              with the other three. . .?

ARTS &
CULTURE   555. ➤ This dish, served at the Passover Seder,
              symbolizes the mortar used by Jewish slaves
              in Egypt . . .?

PEOPLE   556. ➤ What was Israeli Prime Minister Shimon
              Peres originally named at birth. . .?

RELIGION 557. ➤ Moses did this first, but what did Jesus,
              Mohammed and Joseph Smith also all
              have in common. . .?

HISTORY   558. ➤ This racist and anti-Semitic organization
              was originally financed by Judah Ben-
              jamin, a Jewish leader of the Confederacy,
              to fight disorderly elements after the Civil
              War . . .?

LANGUAGE 559. ➤ The Yiddish term *mishmash* means . . .?

GEOGRAPHY 560.➤ Name one of the two minerals besides salt
              which are extracted in large quantities
              from the waters of the Dead Sea. . .?

142

ANSWERS

CURRENT
EVENTS 553 .➤ Two. Hebrew and Arabic.

WOMEN 554. ➤ Rachel. (She was buried in a tomb on the road to Bethlehem.)

ARTS &
CULTURE 555. ➤ Charoses.

PEOPLE 556. ➤ Shimon Persky.

RELIGION 557. ➤ They all claimed to have spoken to God, and then went on to establish major world religions. (Christianity, Islam, Mormonism.)

HISTORY 558. ➤ The Ku Klux Klan (originally it was a protective organization, not the dangerous and racist organization it has now evolved into).

LANGUAGE 559 .➤ Hodgepodge.

GEOGRAPHY560. ➤ Potash and bromide.

Trivia Judaica   QUESTIONS

CURRENT
EVENTS   561. ➤ The seal of the State of Israel is represented by these two symbolic items. . .?

WOMEN   562. ➤ In the Bible, whose family had 12 sons and one daughter. . .?

ARTS &
CULTURE   563. ➤ This Israeli writer won the 1966 Nobel Prize for Literature . . .?

PEOPLE   564. ➤ This Israeli mayor once publicly compared Menachem Begin to Idi Amin. . .?

RELIGION   565. ➤ England's Reform Jewish Movement is called. . .?

HISTORY   566. ➤ This rightwing Zionist youth movement played a key role in the Warsaw Ghetto uprising against the Nazis . . .?

LANGUAGE   567. ➤ The Hebrew word *brit* means . . .?

GEOGRAPHY 568. ➤ The Dead Sea Scrolls and other ancient manuscripts are displayed in this Israeli institution. . .?

ANSWERS

CURRENT
EVENTS 561. ➤ A Menorah (representing the enlightenment of culture) and leaves (representing fruitfulness and peace).

WOMEN 562. ➤ Jacob's.

ARTS &
CULTURE 563. ➤ S. Y. Agnon.

PEOPLE 564. ➤ Mayor Teddy Kollek of Jerusalem.

RELIGION 565. ➤ The Liberal Jewish Union.

HISTORY 566. ➤ *Betar*.

LANGUAGE 567. ➤ Covenant.

GEOGRAPHY 568. ➤ The Shrine of the Book which is part of the Israel Museum, in Jerusalem.

CURRENT
EVENTS   569. ➤ Approximately how many Ph.D's and
               M.D.'s have graduated from Arab run
               Universities in the West Bank, since
               1967. . .?

WOMEN   570. ➤ This Israeli Prime Minister was raised in
               Milwaukee, Wisconsin . . .?

ARTS &
CULTURE   571. ➤ This Jewish film maker directed *All the
               President's Men* and *Sophie's Choice*. . .?

PEOPLE   572. ➤ This writer, who has written some novels
               about Israel, wrote the bestselling novel of
               1976—about Ireland. Name him. . .?

RELIGION 573. ➤ Why is it impossible to seriously believe in
               both Judaism and Communism simulta-
               neously. . .?

HISTORY   574. ➤ How did Adolph Hitler die. . .?

LANGUAGE 575. ➤ The Yiddish word *nosh* refers to . . .?

GEOGRAPHY 576. ➤ This ancient fortress is located in the north-
               ern Galilee, a few miles west of the upper
               Jordan river . . .?

ANSWERS

CURRENT
EVENTS 569. ➤ **None. The media calls them Universities, but they are actually equivalent to two-year colleges, trade schools and terrorist training grounds.**

WOMEN 570. ➤ **Golda Meir.**

ARTS &
CULTURE 571. ➤ **Alan Pakula.**

PEOPLE 572. ➤ **Leon Uris (*Trinity*).**

RELIGION 573. ➤ **Because Communism insists that there is no God, while Judaism was founded on the premise of one God.**

HISTORY 574. ➤ **He committed suicide.**

LANGUAGE 575. ➤ **Food eaten between meals.**

GEOGRAPHY 576. ➤ **Hazor.**

CURRENT
EVENTS   577. ➤ What does AIPAC stand for. . .?

WOMEN   578. ➤ Joyce Bauer, M.D., is known to millions of
                 Americans by what professionl name. . .?

ARTS &
CULTURE   579. ➤ This controversial, lewd Jewish comedian
                 died of a drug overdose in 1966. . .?

PEOPLE   580. ➤ These historic figures had one main thing
                 in common: Mohammed, Pobjedonostew,
                 and Torquemada. . .?

RELIGION   581. ➤ Reform Judaism introduced this ceremony
                 for the young people who attended its
                 religious schools. . .?

HISTORY   582. ➤ Name the two Jews most responsible for
                 creating the Jewish Legion which fought
                 in World War I . . .?

LANGUAGE 583. ➤ The common Hebrew word *ben* translates
                 to . . .?

GEOGRAPHY 584. ➤ This Israeli port is north of Saudi
                 Arabia's. . .?

ANSWERS

CURRENT
EVENTS 577. ➤ **America-Israeli Political Action Committee (Israel's principal lobby in Washington, D.C.).**

WOMEN 578. ➤ **Dr. Joyce Brothers.**

ARTS &
CULTURE 579. ➤ **Lenny Bruce.**

PEOPLE 580. ➤ **Hatred for the Jewish people.**

RELIGION 581. ➤ **The Confirmation Ceremony. (This occurs on *Shavuos*).**

HISTORY 582. ➤ **Joseph Trumpeldor and Ze'ev Jabotinsky.**

LANGUAGE 583. ➤ **Son of.**

GEOGRAPHY 584. ➤ **Eilat.**

CURRENT
EVENTS   585. ➤ Israel has both civil and religious courts. Which cases go before religious courts. . . ?

WOMEN   586. ➤ Who did the Persian King Ahasuerus divorce before marrying Esther. . .?

ARTS &
CULTURE   587. ➤ This Jewish scientist was the only person to ever win two Nobel Prizes . . .?

PEOPLE   588. ➤ This Jewish athlete won gold and silver medals at the Paris Olympics of 1924, and was the subject of the movie *Chariiots of Fire*. . .?

RELIGION   589. ➤ The "Days of Awe" refer to. . .?

HISTORY   590. ➤ He was the only criminal ever to receive capital punishment in the modern State of Israel . . .?

LANGUAGE   591. ➤ The Yiddish term *noodge* refers to . . .?

GEOGRAPHY 592. ➤ The Pillars of Solomon are located at . . .?

ANSWERS

CURRENT
EVENTS 585. ➤ Personal status cases, such as marriage, divorce, etc.

WOMEN 586. ➤ Vashti .

ARTS &
CULTURE 587. ➤ Dr. Linus Pauling (Chemistry in 1954 and the Peace Prize in 1962).

PEOPLE 588. ➤ Harold Abrahams.

RELIGION 589. ➤ The ten days from Rosh Hashanah to Yom Kippur.

HISTORY 590. ➤ Adolf Eidhmann, the Nazi murderer.

LANGUAGE 591. ➤ An annoying person.

GEOGRAPHY 592. ➤ The entrance to the Timna copper mines in Israel's Negev desert.

Trivia Judaica   QUESTIONS

CURRENT
EVENTS   593. ➤ Where is the Israeli swamp which was
               drained by the pioneers, amid song and
               celebration, but is now being reflooded by
               the JNF. . .?

WOMEN   594. ➤ This famous 1946 conference marked a
               turning point for women within Judaism.
               Reform rabbis stated: "It is our sacred duty
               to declare with all emphasis the complete
               religious equality of women" . . .?

ARTS &
CULTURE   595. ➤ This anti-Semitic European dictator was
               Time Magazine's "Man of the Year" in
               1937 . . .?

PEOPLE   596. ➤ Name the Jewish singer/songwriter who
               won and Academy Award for best song of
               1988. . .?

RELIGION 597. ➤ What was the attitude of Isaac Mayer Wise
               and his followers towards the Zionist move-
               ment. . . ?

HISTORY   598. ➤ The name of the acting Chief of the Israeli
               Mossad is never made public. He or she is
               referred to as . . .?

LANGUAGE 599. ➤ A *Zaftig* woman refers to one who is. . .?

GEOGRAPHY 600. ➤ What body of water is found south-west of
               the Sinai. . . ?

ANSWERS

CURRENT
EVENTS   593. ▶ The Hula Valley.

WOMEN   594. ▶ The Breslow Conference.

ARTS &
CULTURE   595. ▶ Adolph Hitler.

PEOPLE   596. ▶ Carly Simon for "Let the River Run."
from *Working Girl.*

RELIGION   597. ▶ They were against it. They believed the
Jewish people formed a religion and
should not try to become a nation.

HISTORY   598. ▶ Number One.

LANGUAGE   599. ▶ A full bodied and well put together
woman.

GEOGRAPHY 600. ▶ The Gulf of Suez.

Trivia Judaica   **QUESTIONS**

CURRENT
EVENTS   601. ▶ Tay-Sachs disease disrupts the functioning of which system of the human body, affecting Jews in higher proportions than Gentiles. . . ?

WOMEN   602. ▶ She was the first woman to become a minister in the Government of Menachem Begin. . .?

ARTS &
CULTURE   603. ▶ These two Jewish comedian-actors won Tony awards for their roles in the 1963 and 1972 productions of *A Funny Thing Happenned On the Way to the Forum*. . .?

PEOPLE   604. ▶ He was an outstanding personality in the U.S. labor movement and in 1932 became president of the International Ladies Garment Workers' Union. . .?

RELIGION 605. ▶ These characteristics identify an animal as kosher. . .?

HISTORY   606. ▶ The British controlled Palestine during these years. . .?

LANGUAGE 607. ▶ *Shalom* is a tricky Hebrew word with these three meanings. . .?

GEOGRAPHY 608. ▶ The first Sephardic Synagogue in the Eastern hemisphere was founded on this island in 1732. . .?

ANSWERS

CURRENT
EVENTS   601. ➤ The nervous system.

WOMEN   602. ➤ Sara Doron, of the Liberal Party (appointed Minister Without Portfolio in 1983).

ARTS &
CULTURE   603. ➤ Zero Mostel and Phil Silvers.

PEOPLE   604. ➤ David Dubinsky.

RELIGION 605. ➤ It must chew its cud and have split hooves.

HISTORY   606. ➤ 1917 to 1948.

LANGUAGE 607. ➤ Hello, goodbye and peace.

GEOGRAPHY 608. ➤ Curacao.

Trivia Judaica   **QUESTIONS**

CURRENT
EVENTS   609. ➤ Branch Davidian self-proclaimed "messiah" David Koresh was versed in Jewish practice. Where did he get his Yeshiva training. . .?

WOMEN   610. ➤ This character actress, known for her kvetchy roles, has won two Oscars. . .?

ARTS &
CULTURE   611. ➤ He was the creator of the "Dick Van Dyke" show and has a son who produces major critically acclaimed movies for Hollywood. . .?

PEOPLE   612. ➤ This Israeli was hanged in Damascus Square in May 1965, for spying and was known by the alias, Kamil Amin Taqbes. He is fondly remembered as "Our Man in Damascus" . . .?

RELIGION 613. ➤ Which modern Christian group is influenced by the idea of a Jewish God. . . ?

HISTORY   614. ➤ Approximately how many Jews of Polish origin perished in the Holocaust . . .?

LANGUAGE 615. ➤ The Hebrew religious term *muktzeh*, refers to. . .?

GEOGRAPHY 616. ➤ In 1940, legislation was introduced in Congress, and then voted down, that would have allowed Jewish refugees to settle in this part of the U.S.. . .?

ANSWERS

CURRENT
EVENTS   609. ➤ He was an unregistered student at several Jerusalem schools, including the *Aish Hatorah* Yeshiva in the old city.

WOMEN   610. ➤ Shelley Winters.

ARTS &
CULTURE   611. ➤ Carl Reiner. (His son is Rob Reiner.)

PEOPLE   612. ➤ Eli Cohen.

RELIGION 613. ➤ The Unitarians.

HISTORY   614. ➤ Three million.

LANGUAGE 615. ➤ Items that should not be touched on the Sabbath or on certain holidays (such as money, machines, work tools, etc.)

GEOGRAPHY616. ➤ Alaska.

Trivia Judaica   QUESTIONS

CURRENT
EVENTS   617. ➤ What organization inspired Black leaders
          and others to condemn the racist speech
          given at Kean College by a leader of
          Farrakhan's "Nation of Islam" organiza-
          tion, and how did they do it. . .?

WOMEN   618. ➤ She played Rebecca, the Jewess, in the
          1952 film version of Walter Scott's
          Ivanhoe. Later she converted to Judaism.
          Name her. . .?

ARTS &
CULTURE   619. ➤ She co-wrote many pop hits and was mar-
          ried to Burt Bacharach. Who is she. . .?

PEOPLE   620. ➤ He was the King of England at the time of
          the Balfour Declaration, which was issued
          on November 29, 1917. . .?

RELIGION 621. ➤ The Ashkenazim call this the *Aron ha-
          Kodesh*, the Sephardim call it *Hei Khal*—
          the place in the synagogue where what is
          kept . . .?

HISTORY   622. ➤ When did Israel and Egypt fight the "War
          of Attrition"?

LANGUAGE 623. ➤ In what language is the traditional Jewish
          wedding contract, the *Ketubah*, written?

GEOGRAPHY 624. ➤ The three largest U.S. Jewish population
          centers are. . .?

ANSWERS

CURRENT
EVENTS 617. ➤ The Anti-Defamation League took out full page ads in newspapers quoting the verbal attacks on Jews, the Pope, Catholics and Whites.

WOMEN 618. ➤ Elizabeth Taylor.

ARTS &
CULTURE 619. ➤ Carole Bayer Sager.

PEOPLE 620. ➤ King George V.

RELIGION 621. ➤ The Ark.

HISTORY 622. ➤ 1969-1970. (While terrorist activity occurred after the Six-Day War, all out fighting erupted in 1969 and continued until the U.S.—mediated cease fire, in 1970.)

LANGUAGE 623. ➤ Aramaic.

GEOGRAPHY 624. ➤ New York City, Los Angeles and Philadelphia. (Chicago and Miami are fourth and fifth.)

CURRENT
EVENTS 625. ➤ Harvard professor John Strugnell was dismissed from stewardship of this major archeological project because of his anti-Semitic remarks. . .?

WOMEN 626. ➤ This book of the Bible, named after a woman, never mentions the name of God. . .?

ARTS &
CULTURE 627. ➤ This Borscht Belt comedian won an Oscar for a movie which starred Marlon Brando. . .?

PEOPLE 628. ➤ This young Jewish lawyer (now deceased) gained fame as Committee Council at the McCarthy hearings of the early 1950's . . .?

RELIGION 629. ➤ How did two Jewish collaborators help Mohammed?

HISTORY 630. ➤ Abba Eban, in describing Israel's pre-1967 borders, compared them to a concentration camp, calling them "_____ Lines". . .?

LANGUAGE 631. ➤ What are the literal and figurative meanings of the Yiddish word *shmaltz*?

GEOGRAPHY 632. ➤ The Levantine Jews come from this area. . .?

ANSWERS

CURRENT
EVENTS 625. ➤ The Dead Sea Scrolls project.

WOMEN 626. ➤ The Book of Esther.

ARTS &
CULTURE 627. ➤ Red Buttons (in *Sayonara*).

PEOPLE 628. ➤ Roy Cohn.

RELIGION 629. ➤ They assisted him in editing the Koran.

HISTORY 630. ➤ *"Auschwitz* Lines"—because they could lead to an even worse tragedy than Auschwitz: the destruction of Israel.

LANGUAGE 631. ➤ Literal: chicken fat.
Figurative: extreme sentimentality.

GEOGRAPHY632. ➤ Asia Minor.

CURRENT
EVENTS   633. ➤ Who was known as the "Junk Bond King". . .?

WOMEN   634. ➤ A Jewish girl becomes *Bat Mitzvah* at this age. . .?

ARTS &
CULTURE   635. ➤ This Jewish comedian played the role of Rufus T. Firefly in his beloved movies. . .?

PEOPLE   636. ➤ This Jewish born thinker founded Socialism. . .?

RELIGION   637. ➤ What is *Shmura* Matzah?

HISTORY   638. ➤ In 1969, this Israeli organization allegedly stole the blueprints for the Mirage III fighter jet from Switzerland. . .?

LANGUAGE 639. ➤ What does *Golem* refer to. . .?

GEOGRAPHY640. ➤ What Jewish Holy city has 110,000 Moslem and 14,000 Christian inhabitants?

ANSWERS

CURRENT
EVENTS   633. ➤ **Michael Milken.**

WOMEN   634. ➤ **Twelve.**

ARTS &
CULTURE   635. ➤ **Groucho Marx.**

PEOPLE   636. ➤ **Karl Marx.**

RELIGION   637. ➤ **Literally, guarded matzah. It is the matzah eaten on Passover by the most pious Jews. (Every stage of the production process is carefully monitored.)**

HISTORY   638. ➤ **The *Mossad*, the Israeli CIA.**

LANGUAGE   639. ➤ **A creation of man that is given life through magical means.**

GEOGRAPHY   640. ➤ **Jerusalem.**

Trivia Judaica   **QUESTIONS**

CURRENT
EVENTS   641. ➤ What is the most outrageous anti-Semitic
              resolution ever passed by the U.N. and in
              what decade was it passed. . . ?

WOMEN   642. ➤ These Jewish twin sisters, with all-Ameri-
              can-sounding adopted names, ironically
              have competing newspaper columns . . .?

ARTS &
CULTURE   643. ➤ David Ricardo was a famous Jewish 19th
              century theoretician known as the father of
              which branch of the social sciences . . .?

PEOPLE   644. ➤ She was the first female in history to be
              elected as head of Government. . .?

RELIGION 645. ➤ During this holiday we say, "And for all of
              them, O God of forgiveness, forgive us"
              . . .?

HISTORY   646. ➤ On the day that Israel declared its indepen-
              dence, Chaim Weizmann and Abba Eban
              were not in Israel. They were both in. . .?

LANGUAGE 647. ➤ The frequently used Yiddish term to de-
              scribe someone who is crazy or mad is . . .?

GEOGRAPHY648. ➤ This river is the longest in Israel . . .?

ANSWERS

CURRENT
EVENTS 641. ➤ **In the 1970's (November 10th, 1975 to be exact), condemning Zionism as a racist movement.**

WOMEN 642. ➤ **Ann Landers (Esther Friedman) and Abigail Van Buren (Pauline Friedman).**

ARTS &
CULTURE 643. ➤ **Economics.**

PEOPLE 644. ➤ **Golda Meir.**

RELIGION 645. ➤ *Yom Kippur.*

HISTORY 646. ➤ **New York City, as Israel's delegates to the United Nations. (Israel was not formally admitted to the U.N. for another year.)**

LANGUAGE 647. ➤ *Meshuggeh* or *Meshuggeneh.*

GEOGRAPHY 648. ➤ **The Jordan.**

Trivia Judaica   Questions

CURRENT
EVENTS   649. ➤ This national Jewish daily newspaper began in the 1990's and is a derivitive of the
longest running Yiddish-language newspaper in the United States. . . ?

WOMEN   650. ➤ This Polish-born Jewish woman built an
empire in the American cosmetics busi-
ness . . .?

ARTS &
CULTURE 651. ➤ Name the Jewish musician who won three
Oscars in 1974. . .?

PEOPLE   652. ➤ This Jewish lawyer was appointed by President Franklin D. Roosevelt to the United
States Supreme Court . . .?

RELIGION 653. ➤ Under these circumstances, some Jewish
parents threaten their adult children that
they will sit *shiva*, even though no one has
died . . .?

HISTORY   654. ➤ On March 16, 1190, there was another
occurrence in Jewish history, besides
Masada—when besieged Jews chose suicide rather than submit to capture and
ignoble death. Where did this happen?

LANGUAGE 655. ➤ On February 24, 1949, Israel and this Arab
nation signed an agreement following the
War of Independence . . ?

GEOGRAPHY 656. ➤ The Nazis planned a major "Museum of
the Extinct Race" in this European city. . .?

ANSWERS

CURRENT
EVENTS 649. ➤ **"The Forward" (which is distributed throughout North America).**

WOMEN 650. ➤ **Helena Rubinstein.**

ARTS &
CULTURE 651. ➤ **Marvin Hamlish (for his music from *The Sting* and *The Way We Were*).**

PEOPLE 652. ➤ **Felix Frankfurter.**

RELIGION 653. ➤ **When a child intermarries or converts from the Jewish religion. (The appropriate thing for the offending children to do in these circumstances is to make a *Shiva* call on their parents!)**

HISTORY 654. ➤ **In York, England. More than 500 Jews chose suicide in the castle where they had sought protection, rather than face certain death at the hands of the anti-Semitic murderous mob outside. (They started a fire inside the castle and all perished.)**

LANGUAGE 655. ➤ **Egypt (signed in Rhodes).**

GEOGRAPHY 656. ➤ **Prague.**

CURRENT
EVENTS   657. ➤ She was the first Jewish female United
                States Senator. . . ?

WOMEN   658. ➤ What is the ancient Hebrew name for a
                marriage contract. . .?

ARTS &
CULTURE   659. ➤ This Jewish tough-guy actor played the
                role of Popeye Doyle, in a popular 1970
                action movie and a lawyer in a popular
                1993-1994 movie. . .?

PEOPLE   660. ➤ This family of Jewish financiers were the
                first to popularize the making of loans to
                nations. . .?

RELIGION 661. ➤ In 1984, these religious authorities issued
                a joint statement asserting that "Reform
                Jews are Jews, just like us". . .?

HISTORY   662. ➤ This tribunal persecuted Jews in Medieval
                Spain. . .?

LANGUAGE 663. ➤ The Hebrew word *Maccabee* translates
                into. . .?

GEOGRAPHY 664. ➤ What did Nelson Glueck discover at Ezion
                Gever . . .?

ANSWERS

CURRENT
EVENTS 657. ➤ **Senator Diane Feinstein, U.S. Senator, California.**

WOMEN 658. ➤ *Ketubah.*

ARTS &
CULTURE 659. ➤ **Gene Hackman (in *The French Connection* and *The Firm*).**

PEOPLE 660. ➤ **The Rothschilds.**

RELIGION 661. ➤ **Israel's two chief rabbis.**

HISTORY 662. ➤ **The Inquisition.**

LANGUAGE 663. ➤ **Hammer.**

GEOGRAPHY 664. ➤ **King Solomon's Mines.**

CURRENT
EVENTS 665. ➤ President Reagan's historic mistake in going to the German military cemetary at Bitburg (where Nazi officers are buried) was compounded by this ill conceived comparison . . .?

WOMEN 666. ➤ She devoted her life to Jewish communal and intellectual activity, working for the Jewish Publication Society and founding this major American women's organization. . .?

ARTS &
CULTURE 667. ➤ In this 1970's movie, Gene Wilder played an Orthodox Jew attempting, among other things, to speak Yiddish to Amish Pennsylvania Dutch farmers wearing long black coats . . .?

PEOPLE 668. ➤ Spain's Francisco Franco felt this way about diplomatic relations with Israel . . .?

RELIGION 669. ➤ The Conservative Movement was originally called. . .?

HISTORY 670. ➤ At what point in Jewish history did the largest numbers of Jews migrate to Holland?

LANGUAGE 671. ➤ The Yiddish and Hebrew term *mashumed* refers to one who has . . .?

GEOGRAPHY672. ➤ The well-known Hassidic rabbi, Levi Yitzhak, was associated with this East European town . . .?

ANSWERS

CURRENT
EVENTS 665. ➤ He equated the murderers and their victims, making the incredible statement that both had suffered equally.

WOMEN 666. ➤ Henrietta Szold.

ARTS &
CULTURE 667. ➤ *The Frisco Kid.*

PEOPLE 668. ➤ Adamant in his insistence that no such ties be established.

RELIGION 669. ➤ Historical Judaism.

HISTORY 670. ➤ After they were expelled from Spain.

LANGUAGE 671. ➤ Converted to Christianity ("a destroyed one").

GEOGRAPHY 672. ➤ Berditchev. (A well-known book was written about him called *Levi Yitzhak of Berditchev*, by Samuel H. Dresner.)

Trivia Judaica   QUESTIONS

CURRENT
EVENTS   673. ➤ What action did France take against the
              organizer of the Munich Olympic massa-
              cre, after he was arrested in Paris, in 1976.
              . . ?

WOMEN   674. ➤ These Jewish women, Anna Pavlova and
              Alicia Markova, have this in common. . .?

ARTS &
CULTURE   675. ➤ The general Jewish view on organ trans-
              plants is . . .?

PEOPLE   676. ➤ He personally donated the largest amount
              of money in history, over $45,000,000 (in
              present dollars, this would be nearly 1
              billion dollars), to resettle the abused Jews
              of Russia in other countries. . .?

RELIGION 677. ➤ What caused Haman to attempt to murder
              the Jews. . .?

HISTORY   678. ➤ What French monarch began the emanci-
              pation of Jews. . .?

LANGUAGE 679. ➤ In Yiddish, when a social match is made
              between two people it is known as a. . .?

GEOGRAPHY 680. ➤ What two nations emerged from the dis-
              mantling of the Turkish Ottoman Empire,
              first as British Mandates in 1921, and later
              as independent nations, in 1932 and 1946?

ANSWERS

CURRENT
EVENTS   673. ➤ They released him, caving in to Arab pressure.

WOMEN   674. ➤ Both were famous ballerinas.

ARTS &
CULTURE   675. ➤ Organ transplants are allowed because saving a human life outweighs all other considerations.

PEOPLE   676. ➤ Baron Maurice de Hirsch.

RELIGION   677. ➤ He was angry because a Jew would not bow down to him.

HISTORY   678. ➤ Napolean.

LANGUAGE   679. ➤ *"Shiddach."*

GEOGRAPHY   680. ➤ Iraq (in 1932) and Transjordan (in 1946).

Trivia Judaica   **QUESTIONS**

CURRENT
EVENTS 681. ➤ What military event became known as
Israel's daring "Operation Babylon," in
the early 80's. . . ?

WOMEN 682. ➤ The Torah describes this dynamic woman
as a great Israelite ruler who led her followers in battle . . .?

ARTS &
CULTURE 683. ➤ He was the Jewish actor who played a
cowboy on an immensely successful TV
series. Who was the other Jewish-born
cowboy in his family on this show?

PEOPLE 684. ➤ The first century Romans called him "King
of the Jews." Who was he and what was his
English and Hebrew Name . . .?

RELIGION 685. ➤ The spiritual leaders of the Ethiopian Jewish community are referred to as . . .?

HISTORY 686. ➤ Egypt's Anwar Sadat visited Israel in this
year. . .?

LANGUAGE 687. ➤ In Yiddish, one who is *ongeblassen* is. . .?

GEOGRAPHY688. ➤ Before 1948, the State of Israel was
called. . .?

ANSWERS

CURRENT
EVENTS   681. ➤ **The destruction of Iraq's nuclear reactor in Osirak, deep in Iraqi territory. (Israeli planes made the long distance raid, refeuling in mid-air).**

WOMEN   682. ➤ **Deborah.**

ARTS &
CULTURE   683. ➤ **Lorne Greene and Michael Landon, in "Bonanza." (The late Michael Landon was half-Jewish.)**

PEOPLE   684. ➤ **Jesus (in Hebrew, Yehoshua).**

RELIGION   685. ➤ **Kess (the equivalent of a rabbi—known in Ethiopia as Jewish High Priests).**

HISTORY   686. ➤ **1977.**

LANGUAGE 687. ➤ **Conceited or arrogant.**

GEOGRAPHY 688. ➤ **Palestine.**

Trivia Judaica   QUESTIONS

CURRENT
EVENTS   689. ➤ Israel's "Bar Lev" line refers to. . . ?

WOMEN   690. ➤ This humorous old-time Jewish actress-comic refers to her husband as "Fang", while performing her act . . .?

ARTS &
CULTURE   691. ➤ This Jewish songwriter composed one of the most popular Christmas songs ever written. . .?

PEOPLE   692. ➤ This American business giant printed the forged *Protocols of the Elders of Zion* in a newspaper he owned and regularly promoted stories about Jewish conspiracies to take over America. . .?

RELIGION   693. ➤ The very first sentence of the Bible is. . .?

HISTORY   694. ➤ This world event precipitated the collapse of the Ottoman-Turkish empire. . .?

LANGUAGE 695. ➤ The Yiddish term to describe all of one s relatives is . . .?

GEOGRAPHY 696. ➤ In 1935, these three nations had the largest Jewish populations in the world. . .?

ANSWERS

689. ➤ Israeli fortifications on the Sinai side of the Suez Canal, built after the Six-Day War and named after General Bar Lev.

WOMEN 690. ➤ Phyllis Diller.

ARTS &
CULTURE 691. ➤ Irving Berlin. (The song is "White Christmas").

PEOPLE 692. ➤ Henry Ford, in the 1920's.

RELIGION 693. ➤ "In the beginning God created the heaven and the earth."

HISTORY 694. ➤ World War I.

LANGUAGE 695. ➤ *Mishpocheh.*

GEOGRAPHY 696. ➤ The U.S., the Soviet Union and Poland.

CURRENT
EVENTS   697. ➤ Moderate Arab leaders now recognize that
               Israel is not their primary enemy; rather
               their most serious threat comes from this
               movement . . .?

WOMEN   698. ➤ This Jewish entertainer is dubbed "the
               Divine Miss M". . .?

ARTS &
CULTURE 699. ➤ Why is it highly likely that William
               Shakespeare had never seen a Jew in his
               life when he wrote *The Merchant Of
               Venice*. . .?

PEOPLE   700. ➤ This Jewish female poet originated the
               poem inscribed on the Statue of Liberty,
               that included these words: "Huddled masses
               yearning to breathe free". . .?

RELIGION 701. ➤ The largest Orthodox Jewish religious or-
               ganization in the United States is . . .?

HISTORY   702. ➤ When Jews first arrived in the New World,
               this British politician based in the New
               World who was Governor of New York,
               requested that the board of directors of the
               West India Company "Require them in a
               friendly way to depart . . . that the deceitful
               race . . . be not allowed further to infect
               and trouble their new colony" . . .?

LANGUAGE 703. ➤ What is the Hebrew word for Israel's
               equivalent of the Central Intelligence
               Agency. . .?

GEOGRAPHY 704. ➤ This city was the capital of ancient Israel
               when the Kingdom was divided . . .?

ANSWERS

CURRENT
EVENTS   697. ➤ *Hammas,* known as the "Party Of God," an extreme, murderous Muslim Fundamentalist group.

WOMEN   698. ➤ Bette Midler.

ARTS &
CULTURE   699. ➤ Because the Jews of England had been expelled at that time (in 1290).

PEOPLE   700. ➤ Emma Lazarus.

RELIGION   701. ➤ The Union of Orthodox Jewish Congregations of America.

HISTORY   702. ➤ Governor Peter Stuyvesant. (A counterpetition was made by Portuguese Jews who were principal stockholders in the company, and this persuaded the directors to refuse the request.)

LANGUAGE   703. ➤ The *Mossad,* which handles foreign intelligence operations.

GEOGRAPHY   704. ➤ Shechem.

CURRENT
EVENTS   705. ➤ Why are some Ultra-Orthodox Jews opposed to the State of Israel and its governing law. . . ?

WOMEN   706. ➤ Most of this Jewish talk-show host and
comedienne's jokes are about herself. She
changed her name from Molinsky and had
a husband named Edgar . . . ?

ARTS &
CULTURE 707. ➤ Why do charitable donations from Jewish
sources often come in multiples of 18. . .?

PEOPLE   708. ➤ The great Jewish writer I.L.Peretz was
born in this country—and his initials stand
for. . .?

RELIGION 709. ➤ When, if ever, did Moses enter the Promised Land?

HISTORY   710. ➤ The Jewish people were forced to wear an
identifying badge for the very first time
by. . .?

LANGUAGE 711. ➤ Territorialists and Zionists differed regarding this aspect of the eventual
georaphic location of the Jewish homeland. . .?

GEOGRAPHY712. ➤ The ancient name for the Land of Israel
was. . .?

ANSWERS

CURRENT
EVENTS 705. ➤ Because they believe that a homeland
for the Jewish people can only be created by the coming of the Messiah, and
that the laws governing a Jewish homeland should come from the Torah and
Talmud and not be created through
Knesset votes.

WOMEN 706. ➤ Joan Rivers (born Joan Molinsky).

ARTS &
CULTURE 707. ➤ Eighteen in Hebrew letters spells *chai*,
meaning life. Thus, gifts in this multiple
are considered "gifts of life".

PEOPLE 708. ➤ Poland. His name was Itzhak Leib
Peretz. (His descendant is the publisher
of *The New Republic*, Martin Peretz.)

RELIGION 709. ➤ Never—he was in sight of it when he
died.

HISTORY 710. ➤ Caliph Omar II (in the 9th Century).

LANGUAGE 711. ➤ Territorialists would accept any practical area that was available, while Zion-
ists would only accept Palestine as a
legitimate homeland for the Jewish
people.

GEOGRAPHY 712. ➤ Cannan.

CURRENT
EVENTS   713. ► What did Israel's Rina Mor-Messinger do on July 11th, 1976, that made her a first...?

WOMEN   714. ► The Friedman sisters are otherwise known by their famous newspaper advice column names...?

ARTS &
CULTURE   715. ► This is the language spoken by most Jews in the world today...?

PEOPLE   716. ► What did Victor Kugler do to distinguish himself as a "righteous Gentile"...?

RELIGION 717. ► This Jewish holiday is often considered as the basis for the first ancient Jewish contribution to the art form known as "the drama"...?

HISTORY   718. ► The Spanish Inquisition refers specifically to...?

LANGUAGE 719. ► The uncomplimentary Yiddish term *Nishtgootnick* refers to...?

GEOGRAPHY 720.► Most of the Jews in the world live in these three countries...?

ANSWERS

713. ➤ She became the first entrant from Israel to win the Miss Universe title.

WOMEN 714. ➤ Ann Landers and Abigail Van Buren.

ARTS &
CULTURE 715. ➤ English.

PEOPLE 716. ➤ He hid the family of Anne Frank for 25 months.

RELIGION 717. ➤ The Purim celebration and its dramatization of the story of Haman and Esther.

HISTORY 718. ➤ Religious courts to punish Jews for practicing their religion.

LANGUAGE 719. ➤ A good-for-nothing.

GEOGRAPHY 720. ➤ The United States, Israel and the former Soviet Union.

Trivia Judaica   **QUESTIONS**

CURRENT
EVENTS 721. ➤ Iraq's biggest financial supporter in its war
with Israel used to be . . .?

WOMEN   722. ➤ Why would an instant *cholent* be highly
unlikely?

ARTS &
CULTURE 723. ➤ This actor turned director guided Kathy
Bates to an Oscar for the film *Misery*. Who
is he and what TV sit-com did he appear in
for 6 years. . .?

PEOPLE   724. ➤ In 1958, this Israeli Foreign Minister said,
"Is the world really asking too much if it
demands of this vast Arab empire that it
live in peace and harmony with a little
state, established in the cradle of its birth
. . . within the narrowest territory in which
its natural purposes can ever be fulfilled
. . . "?

RELIGION 725. ➤ New York's Jewish Theological Seminary
is affiliated with this denomination within
Judaism . . .?

HISTORY   726. ➤ In 1891, the Jews of Corfu, Greece, were
aggrieved by this spurious and often used
accusation, popular with Jew-haters
throughout history. . .?

LANGUAGE 727. ➤ Who are the *yordim*. . . ?

GEOGRAPHY728. ➤ In what body of water are the Abu Rudez
oil fields. . . ?

ANSWERS

CURRENT
EVENTS   721. ➤ **Saudi Arabia. (They have now seen the light).**

WOMEN   722. ➤ **By definition, and through 1000's of years of Jewish history, it is supposed to stew all night because of the prohibition against cooking on the Sabbath. (Instant versions would be ridiculed.)**

ARTS &
CULTURE   723. ➤ **Rob Reiner. He appeared in *All In The Family* as a "Meat Head".**

PEOPLE   724. ➤ **Abba Eban.**

RELIGION   725. ➤ **Conservative.**

HISTORY   726. ➤ **They were accused of blood libel (using the blood of Christian children to make their *matzohs*).**

LANGUAGE   727. ➤ **Israelis who emigrate permanently. The word literally means "one who has descended" and is used perjoritively.**

GEOGRAPHY   728. ➤ **The Gulf of Suez.**

CURRENT
EVENTS   729. ➤ What was Israel's "Operation Redemption" on July 4th, 1976. . . ?

WOMEN   730. ➤ This Jewish actress won an Academy Award for Best Supporting Actress in *The Diary of Anne Frank*. Her real last name is Schrift . . .?

ARTS &
CULTURE   731. ➤ This Jewish comedian wrote and directed the soon-to-be released movie *Blazing Saddles Two*. . .?

PEOPLE   732. ➤ He is Israel's greatest tennis player . . .?

RELIGION 733. ➤ A famous Biblical proverb suggests this is the best way to answer a fool . . .?

HISTORY   734. ➤ During the War of Independence, Egypt recalled troops threatening Jerusalem and redeployed them in preparation for an Israeli offensive in the Negev. This happened because reconnaissance planes reported a major build-up of Israeli forces. Israeli forces were actually assembled to listen to what . . .?

LANGUAGE 735. ➤ The uncomplimentary Yiddish term *nachshlepper* describes one who . . .?

GEOGRAPHY 736. ➤ This Jewish food item is named after the Russian City of Bialystock. . .?

ANSWERS

CURRENT
EVENTS 729. ➤ **The raid on Entebbe Airport to rescue the hostages taken prisoner by Arab prisoners.**

WOMEN 730. ➤ **Shelley Winters (born Shirley Schrift).**

ARTS &
CULTURE 731. ➤ **Mel Brooks.**

PEOPLE 732. ➤ **Shlomo Glickstein.**

RELIGION 733. ➤ **According to his own folly.**

HISTORY 734. ➤ **A Leonard Bernstein open air concert that 4,000 IDF soldiers travelled to attend—to celebrate the liberation of Beersheba.**

LANGUAGE 735. ➤ **Follows after or hangs on to.**

GEOGRAPHY 736. ➤ **A Bialy.**

Trivia Judaica   QUESTIONS

CURRENT
EVENTS   737. ➤ Jews comprise what percent of the population of the United States?

WOMEN   738. ➤ This Jewish actress is the daughter of a noted actor born Bernard Schwartz and famous for acting under his screen name. She gained fame as a star of horror films and uses her father's adopted last name . . .?

ARTS &
CULTURE   739. ➤ Name the Jewish actress who was raised in an Orthodox Jewish home and stars in a recent movie set in the U.K., opposite Anthony Hopkins . . .?

PEOPLE   740. ➤ Senator Jacob Javits succeeded this other Jewish New York Senator . . .?

RELIGION   741. ➤ A *Machzor* is used on . . .?

HISTORY   742. ➤ The *Haganah* began by representing the entire Jewish community of Palestine. Two new organizations subsequently evolved from its membership. What were they called?

LANGUAGE 743. ➤ The *Yiddish* expression *nu* translates into the English exclamation . . .?

GEOGRAPHY 744. ➤ These four countries border Israel. . .?

ANSWERS

CURRENT
EVENTS   **737.** ➤ **2.5 percent.**

WOMEN   **738.** ➤ **Jamie Lee Curtis (daughter of Tony Curtis).**

ARTS &
CULTURE **739.** ➤ **Debra Winger. (The movie was *Remains of the Day*).**

PEOPLE   **740.** ➤ **Senator Herbert Lehman.**

RELIGION   **741.** ➤ **High Holy Days and for festival prayers.**

HISTORY   **742.** ➤ **The "Irgun" and the "Lechi."**

LANGUAGE **743.** ➤ **Well! or So!**

GEOGRAPHY **744.** ➤ **Lebanon, Syria, Jordan and Egypt.**

Trivia Judaica   QUESTIONS

CURRENT
EVENTS   745. ➤ Three major security and political issues
                 still confronting Israel since the 1967 Six-
                 Day War are. . . ?

WOMEN   746. ➤ Sherry Lansing, of Jewish birth, was the
                 first American woman to ever achieve this
                 position in this industry. . .?

ARTS &
CULTURE   747. ➤ Eliezer Ban Yehuda is most noted for this
                 compilation and writing . . .?

PEOPLE   748. ➤ *On The Town* and *Kaddish* are among this
                 Jewish composer's most celebrated
                 works. . .?

RELIGION   749. ➤ According to the Talmud, this is the best
                 cure for all ailments . . .?

HISTORY   750. ➤ Recalling his visit to the Hurva Synagogue
                 in Jerusalem in 1920, this Englishman
                 said: "That day, they saw for the first time
                 since the destruction of the Temple, a
                 Governor in the land of Palestine who was
                 one of their people. They saw it as the
                 fulfillment of an ancient prophecy". . .?

LANGUAGE   751. ➤ The Talmudic title *Rabenu* means . . .?

GEOGRAPHY   752. ➤ Most of America's earliest Reform Jews
                 come from this country . . .?

ANSWERS

CURRENT
EVENTS 745. ➤ **Secure and internationally recognized borders; Arab recognition of Israel and a lasting peace treaty.**

WOMEN 746. ➤ **The first woman president of a major Hollywood movie studio.**

ARTS &
CULTURE 747. ➤ *The Dictionary of Ancient and Modern Hebrew* (Ehud Ben-Yehuda's pocket dictionary).

PEOPLE 748. ➤ **Leonard Bernstein.**

RELIGION 749. ➤ **Studying the Torah.**

HISTORY 750. ➤ **Sir Herbert Samuel (first High Com issioner of Palestine).**

LANGUAGE 751. ➤ **Our Master or Our Teacher. (It was given to Patriarchs and Presidents of the Sanhedrin.)**

GEOGRAPHY 752. ➤ **Germany.**

CURRENT
EVENTS 753. ➤ How frequently are Israeli elections held and are there any exceptions. . . ?

WOMEN 754. ➤ Molly Picon and Stella Adler both started their acting careers in this ethnic genre. . .?

ARTS &
CULTURE 755. ➤ In what publication is the first printed history of the Jews in the United States found?

PEOPLE 756. ➤ Bobby Fischer beat this Soviet Jew for the Chess Championship of the world. . .?

RELIGION 757. ➤ The Talmud calls this Jewish holiday "One long day" . . .?

HISTORY 758. ➤ In the Paris Peace Conference of 1919, what Agreement regarding the future of the Palestine area was abandoned?

LANGUAGE 759. ➤ The Yiddish adjective *oysgematert* means. . .?

GEOGRAPHY 760. ➤ This city is the highest in Israel . . .?

ANSWERS

CURRENT
EVENTS 753. ➤ **They are supposed to take place every four years, but Parliament can be dissolved at any time, and new elections called.**

WOMEN 754. ➤ **The Yiddish theater.**

ARTS &
CULTURE 755. ➤ *The Farmer's Almanac.* **(The 1793 edition mentions Jews but much of the information was incorrect or anti-Semitic.)**

PEOPLE 756. ➤ **Boris Spassky.**

RELIGION 757. ➤ *Rosh Hashanah.*

HISTORY 758. ➤ **The Sykes-Picot Agreement (for the re distribution of land in the former Ottoman Empire).**

LANGUAGE 759. ➤ **Fatigued.**

GEOGRAPHY 760. ➤ **Safed (at 960 meters).**

Trivia Judaica　　　　　　　　**QUESTIONS**

CURRENT
EVENTS　761. ➤ What is the name of the most recent Is-
raeli-manufactured tank. . . ?

WOMEN　762. ➤ This character actress has played quirky
comic roles, but was nominated for an
Academy Award for her portrayal of a
Jewish immigrant wife on the Lower East
Side in *Hester Street*.

ARTS &
CULTURE 763. ➤ This Jewish artist is best known for her
massive abstract sculpture. Her famous
Homage to the Six Million is in the collection of the Israel Museum . . . ?

PEOPLE　764. ➤ She was the only Jewish "Miss
America". . . ?

RELIGION 765. ➤ "The Beast," mentioned in the Book of
Revelation, is interpreted by some as referring to this Country . . . ?

HISTORY　766. ➤ What was the successful argument used by
a 17th Century Rabbi to persuade Cromwell
to allow the Jews to re-enter England. . . ?

LANGUAGE 767. ➤ The Hebrew-Yiddish word *Golem*
means. . . ?

GEOGRAPHY768. ➤ Roman Vishniac created a famous photo-
journal about this country before the Holocaust . . . ?

ANSWERS

CURRENT
EVENTS 761. ➤ *"Merkava"* or the Chariot tank.

WOMEN 762. ➤ Carol Kane.

ARTS &
CULTURE 763. ➤ Louise Nevelson.

PEOPLE 764. ➤ Bess Meyerson (in 1945).

RELIGION 765. ➤ The Soviet Union.

HISTORY 766. ➤ The Book of David prophesied that there
could be no redemption until the Jews
had been scattered from one end of the
earth to the other and, therefore, until
they were allowed back into England
there could never be a "Last Judgement."

LANGUAGE 767. ➤ A lifeless creation or a clay figure that
cannot speak.

GEOGRAPHY 768. ➤ Poland. (It was called *"A Vanished
World."*)

Trivia Judaica   QUESTIONS

CURRENT
EVENTS   769. ➤ Why are native-born Israelis called *Sabras*.
              . . ?

WOMEN   770. ➤ The 1911 fire that killed 146 garment
              workers, most of them young Jewish
              women, became known as . . .?

ARTS &
CULTURE   771. ➤ This Hebrew king is found in Oscar Wilde's
              Salome. . .?

PEOPLE   772. ➤ What was the tone of most of Sholom
              Aleichem's works. . .?

RELIGION 773. ➤ The ten plagues are mentioned in the Bible
              and in this other liturgical book . . .?

HISTORY   774. ➤ Where, and in what year, did the famous
              Jewish revolt against the Nazi's take
              place. . .?

LANGUAGE 775. ➤ This Hebrew letter also represents the num-
              ber one (1) . . .?

GEOGRAPHY776. ➤ In Biblical times the term Diaspora re-
              ferred to this place . . .?

ANSWERS

CURRENT
EVENTS   769. ➤ A *"Sabra"* is a cactus fruit and, like this fruit, Israelis are said to be tough on the surface and soft and sweet on the inside.

WOMEN   770. ➤ The Triangle Shirtwaist Company Fire.

ARTS &
CULTURE   771. ➤ Herod.

PEOPLE   772. ➤ Humorous.

RELIGION   773. ➤ *The Haggadah.*

HISTORY   774. ➤ The Warsaw Ghetto Uprising, occurred in 1943.

LANGUAGE 775. ➤ *Aleph.*

GEOGRAPHY 776. ➤ Egypt.

CURRENT
EVENTS   777. ➤ How many members are there in the Israeli Knesset. . . ?

WOMEN   778. ➤ This actress was born as Betty Jean Perske and is a first cousin to Israel's Shimon Peres. . . ?

ARTS &
CULTURE   779. ➤ Who was the original Tevye, in the Broadway production of *Fiddler On The Roof.* . .?

PEOPLE   780. ➤ He was the venerable Jewish Conductor of the Boston Pops Orchestra . . .?

RELIGION   781. ➤ The *mitzvah* of *Bikur Cholim* means. . .?

HISTORY   782. ➤ This organization was formed in 1939 to coordinate the fundraising activities of: the United Palestine Appeal, the American Joint Distribution Committee, and the National Refugee Service. . .?

LANGUAGE 783. ➤ The Yiddish word *handlen* means to. . .?

GEOGRAPHY 784. ➤ In recent history, Jewish agricultural settlements were started in this non-Mideast location . . .?

ANSWERS

CURRENT
EVENTS 777. ➤ 120.

WOMEN 778. ➤ Lauren Bacall.

ARTS &
CULTURE 779. ➤ Zero Mostel.

PEOPLE 780. ➤ Arthur Fiedler.

RELIGION 781. ➤ Visitation of the ill and infirmed. (This is a highly personal *"Mitzvah." Bikur Cholim* societies exist in every U.S. city.)

LANGUAGE 782. ➤ Haggle over price or to do business.

GEOGRAPHY 783. ➤ Argentina.

Trivia Judaica   **QUESTIONS**

CURRENT
EVENTS 785. ➤ In the early 1980's, what controversy tran-
spired between the Sandinista government
of Nicaragua and their 50-member Jewish
community. . . ?

WOMEN 786. ➤ This Jewish film star was the first sex
symbol in movie history . . .?

ARTS &
CULTURE 787. ➤ Michaelangelo created a statue of this
Jewish Biblical hero that is displayed in
Florence, Italy. . .?

PEOPLE 788. ➤ He was President Kennedy's Jewish Secretary of Health and later became a U.S.
Senator from Connecticut. . .?

RELIGION 789. ➤ Name the two largest Hassidic groups in
the United States . . .?

HISTORY 790. ➤ This Biblical character was known for his
courage. . .?

LANGUAGE 791. ➤ The Yiddish expressions *Goyishe Kop* and
Goyishe mazel mean . . .?

GEOGRAPHY 792. ➤ What is the approximate Jewish population of Puerto Rico. . . ?

ANSWERS

CURRENT
EVENTS   785. ▶ **The Sandinista government forced the Jewish community into exile, confiscated all Jewish properties, and took over Managua's Synagogue.**

WOMEN   786. ▶ **Theda Bara.**

ARTS &
CULTURE   787. ▶ **David.**

PEOPLE   788. ▶ **Abraham Ribicoff.**

RELIGION   789 . ▶ *Lubavitch* **and** *Satmar.*

HISTORY   790. ▶ **David.**

LANGUAGE 791. ▶ **"Gentile-head" meaning stupid or naive; "gentile-luck" meaning undeserved good fortune.**

GEOGRAPHY 792. ▶ **2,000.**

Trivia Judaica   **QUESTIONS**

CURRENT
EVENTS   793. ➤ This famous Jewish public servant negotiated for the U.S. in the first SALT talks
with the Russians. . . ?

WOMEN   794. ➤ In 1972, Sally Priesand achieved acclaim
in the Reform movement for this reason
. . .?

ARTS &
CULTURE   795. ➤ The Billy Rose Sculpture Garden is next to
this Museum in Israel . . .?

PEOPLE   796. ➤ He founded the Reform Jewish movement
in America. . .?

RELIGION   797. ➤ What is the main effect of Reform Judaism
on "Jewish ceremonial practices"?

HISTORY   798. ➤ The UN divided Palestine into what even-
tually became Israel and Jordan in this
year . . .?

LANGUAGE   799. ➤ The commonly used Yiddish word to describe a fine and admirable person is. . .?

GEOGRAPHY 800. ➤ During World War II, this European country—which had long been considered an
enemy of the Jews due to its anti-Semitic
history—ironically saved many from death
at the hands of the Nazis. . .?

ANSWERS

CURRENT
EVENTS   793. ➤ **Henry Kissinger.**

WOMEN   794. ➤ **She became their first female rabbi.**

ARTS &
CULTURE   795. ➤ **The Israel Museum.**

PEOPLE   796. ➤ **Isaac Mayer Wise.**

RELIGION   797. ➤ **It simplifies and dispenses with those traditions that, according to Reform interpretations, lack contemporary importance.**

HISTORY   798. ➤ **1947 (November 29th).**

LANGUAGE   799. ➤ **A *mensch*.**

GEOGRAPHY   800. ➤ **Spain. (Many Sephardic Jews who had previously applied for Spanish citizenship or who had appeared on embassy lists as former Spanish subjects were saved. Some families had not visited Spain for 500 years.)**

Trivia Judaica   **QUESTIONS**

CURRENT
EVENTS   801. ➤ What are the two types of legal courts
                found in Israel. . . ?

WOMEN   802. ➤ What is symbolized by the two cups of
                wine at a wedding ceremony, that both the
                bride and groom drink from. . . ?

ARTS &
CULTURE   803. ➤ This popular American sport is not played
                in Israel . . . ?

PEOPLE   804. ➤ This Jewish author started the growth in-
                dustry of "futurism" with his 1970 bestseller
                . . . ?

RELIGION 805 ➤ When Israel was part of the Roman Em-
                pire, why did the Sages change the time of
                the Shofar blowing-from the morning to
                the evening?

HISTORY   806. ➤ The PLO terrorist organization was
                founded in this year . . . ?

LANGUAGE 807. ➤ The Hebrew and Yiddish word *Melamed*
                translates to . . . ?

GEOGRAPHY 808. ➤ How exactly would power be generated
                from the "Mediterranean to the Dead Sea"
                canal project that has been halted due to
                lack of funding. . . ?

ANSWERS

CURRENT
EVENTS   801. ➤ Civil courts and Religious courts.

WOMEN   802. ➤ The cups of joy and sorrow, demonstrating their willingness to remain together no matter what life may bring.

ARTS &
CULTURE   803. ➤ Ice hockey (for good reason: no ice).

PEOPLE   804. ➤ Alvin Toffler in *"Future Shock."*

RELIGION   805. ➤ Suspicious Roman authorities, fearful of Jewish uprisings, once interpreted the morning Shofar blasts as a call to arms- so they attacked a synagogue, killing all of the worshippers.

HISTORY   806 ➤ 1964.

LANGUAGE   807. ➤ A teacher or a wise man.

GEOGRAPHY 808. ➤ From the more than 1,000-feet drop from Mediterranean Sea level to Dead Sea level. (The water would go through turbines generating electricity.)

CURRENT
EVENTS 809. ➤ Israeli demographers estimate that by the year 2025 the Jewish population of the Diaspora will drop to (within the nearest million) . . .?

WOMEN 810. ➤ The first romance in the Bible was between. . . ?

ARTS &
CULTURE 811. ➤ He is referred to as the "Poet of the Hebraic (Language) Renaissance" . . .?

PEOPLE 812. ➤ This Jewish family owns the richest Jewish oil fortune in the world. . . ?

RELIGION 813. ➤ What are the three major ancient divisions of the Jewish tribes. . . ?

HISTORY 814. ➤ Bedouin shepherds discovered how many 2,000-year-old Dead Sea Scrolls. . .?

LANGUAGE 815. ➤ In both Yiddish and Hebrew the word *letz* means one who is . . .?

GEOGRAPHY 816. ➤ This town, once a great seat of Jewish learning, is the oldest in the Upper Galilee . . .?

ANSWERS

CURRENT
EVENTS   809. ➤ **5 million people.**

WOMEN   810. ➤ **Jacob and Rachael.**

ARTS &
CULTURE   811. ➤ **Chaim Nachman Bialik.**

PEOPLE   812. ➤ **The Marvin Davis family.**

RELIGION   813. ➤ **The Levites, the Kohanites, and the Israelites.**

HISTORY   814. ➤ **Seven (in 1947).**

LANGUAGE   815. ➤ **A cynic or a comic.**

GEOGRAPHY   816. ➤ **Safed.**

Trivia Judaica — QUESTIONS

CURRENT
EVENTS   817. ➤ Representatives of the Orthodox community in Israel have called for a law which would ban the raising, marketing and sale of this food . . .?

WOMEN   818. ➤ King Solomon was alleged to have had an "affair" with this African queen . . .?

ARTS &
CULTURE 819. ➤ This Jewish actor starred in a spin-off sitcom that developed from "The Mary Tyler Moore Show". . . ?

PEOPLE   820. ➤ This Canadian Jewish family had one of the richest real estate fortunes in the world and then they sought bankruptcy protection in 1993. . . ?

RELIGION 821. ➤ Jews that converted to Christianity against their will were known as . . .?

HISTORY 822. ➤ The "Righteous of the Nations" refers to whom?

LANGUAGE 823. ➤ What does *Torah* mean?

GEOGRAPHY 824. ➤ According to tradition, the geographic location known as "Elijah's Cave" is where the Prophet Elijah took shelter during his flight from the King of Israel. Where in Israel is this Jewish holy site?

ANSWERS

EVENTS   817. ▶ Pork.

WOMEN   818. ▶ The Queen of Sheba. (This is one explanation for the existence of Ethiopian Jews.)

ARTS &
CULTURE   819. ▶ Ed Asner (in Lou Grant).

PEOPLE   820. ▶ The Reichman family (but don't worry, they're still reportedly worth around 1 *billion* dollars).

RELIGION   821. ▶ "The Marranos."

HISTORY   822. ▶ The individuals and governments that helped save Jewish lives during the Holocaust.

LANGUAGE   823. ▶ Law.

GEOGRAPHY 824. ▶ In Haifa on Mt. Carmel.

Trivia Judaica   **QUESTIONS**

CURRENT
EVENTS   825. ➤ What is predicted to be Israel's most seri-
                 ous environmental crisis since the found-
                 ing of the State. . . ?

WOMEN   826. ➤ She is a prominent Jewish film and drama
                 critic, based in New York City, with a very
                 un-Jewish sounding, adopted last name. . .?

ARTS &
CULTURE   827. ➤ This Jewish author wrote: *The Victim,
                 Herzog, Humboldt's Gift* and *Mr.
                 Sammler's Planet*. . .?

PEOPLE   828. ➤ This Jewish businessman led CBS through
                 most of its growth and this other Jewish
                 businessman recently bought a controlling
                 interest in the network. . .?

RELIGION   829. ➤ How many types of labor are traditionally
                 prohibited on the Sabbath?

HISTORY   830. ➤ This Persian king said: " . . . the Lord, the
                 God of heaven, hath given me, and he has
                 charged me to build a house in Jerusalem,
                 which is in Judah". . .?

LANGUAGE   831. ➤ In Yiddish, the not-so-nice expression
                 kochleffel means one who is . . .?

GEOGRAPHY   832. ➤ What are the names of the twin lakes
                 which form part of the Suez Canal?

ANSWERS

CURRENT
EVENTS 825. ➤ **Water. The receding water table is getting worse due to the new demands by all of the added settlers and new industry.**

WOMEN 826. ➤ **Judith Crist (born Judith Klein).**

ARTS &
CULTURE 827. ➤ **Saul Bellow.**

PEOPLE 828. ➤ **William Paley and then Lawrence Tish.**

RELIGION 829. ➤ **Thirty-nine.**

HISTORY 830. ➤ **King Cyrus, when he invited the Jewish people to return to Israel and rebuild the holy Temple.**

LANGUAGE 831. ➤ **A busybody and creates trouble.**

GEOGRAPHY 832. ➤ **The Great Bitter Lake and The Little Bitter Lake.**

CURRENT
EVENTS   833. ➤ What is the most serious and dangerous aspect of the recent terrorist plots against the U.S. . .?

WOMEN   834. ➤ Why was Lot's life turned into a pillar of salt. . . ?

ARTS &
CULTURE   835. ➤ Which prolific Jewish author has the longest entry in *Who's Who In America* because of the numerous (mostly fiction) books he has written. . . ?

PEOPLE   836. ➤ This Jewish-born intellectual with radical ideas said, "Religion is the opiate of the masses. . .?

RELIGION   837. ➤ What was the reasoning behind the ancient Hebrew's disgust with idolatrous religions. . .?

HISTORY   838. ➤ Theodor Herzl first visited Jerusalem in this year (within 5 years accuracy). . .?

LANGUAGE 839. ➤ The 5 Books of Moses were written in this language . . .?

GEOGRAPHY 840. ➤ What famous Jewish institution of higher learning is located in the Washington Heights section of New York City. . .?

ANSWERS

CURRENT
EVENTS 833. ➤ **There is indisputable evidence that the terrorists are state sponsored by radical Islamist states, and are not working independantly or for their own organizations. (The World Trade Center bombing was directed, funded and sponsered by Iran, supported by Libya, and assisted by Sudan).**

WOMEN 834. ➤ **She looked back at the destruction of Sodom.**

ARTS &
CULTURE 835. ➤ **Isaac Asimov.**

PEOPLE 836. ➤ **Karl Marx.**

RELIGION 837. ➤ **They viewed idolatry as linked to immoral practices and behavior.**

HISTORY 838. ➤ **1898.**

LANGUAGE 839. ➤ **Hebrew.**

GEOGRAPHY 840. ➤ **Yeshiva University.**

Trivia Judaica   **QUESTIONS**

CURRENT
EVENTS 841. ➤ Jews represent only 1 percent of the population in Great Britain, but they make up what % of the membership of the Royal Academy of Science (within 2% accuracy). . . ?

WOMEN 842. ➤ He had 1,000 wives, according to the book of Kings. . . ?

ARTS &
CULTURE 843. ➤ Honey is eaten on challah especially during this time of the year. . .?

PEOPLE 844. ➤ This Jewish composer took Scott Joplin tunes and turned them into an Academy Award-winning film score . . .?

RELIGION 845. ➤ What are the 4 main ingredients of *charoseth*?

HISTORY 846. ➤ He was a soldier in the British Army nicknamed "Lawrence of Judea" who trained members of the *Haganah* so that they could protect the oil pipeline from Iraq to Haifa . . .?

LANGUAGE 847. ➤ The not-so-nice Yiddish and Hebrew term *Kamtsan* means . . .?

GEOGRAPHY 848. ➤ A princess from this Arab country was publicly beheaded in 1977, when she attempted to flee the country with her boyfriend, a commoner. . .?

ANSWERS

CURRENT
EVENTS   **841.** ➤ **7 percent.**

WOMEN   **842.** ➤ **Solomon.**

ARTS &
CULTURE   **843.** ➤ **From "Rosh Hashanah" to "Yom Kippur."**

PEOPLE   **844.** ➤ **Marvin Hamlisch.**

RELIGION   **845.** ➤ **Apples, almonds, cinnamon and wine—mixed together (eaten during the Passover Seder).**

HISTORY   **846.** ➤ **Charles Orde Wingate**

LANGUAGE   **847.** ➤ **A stingy tightwad.**

GEOGRAPHY **848.** ➤ **Saudi Arabia.**

CURRENT
EVENTS   849. ➤ The two major political parties in Israel
are. . . ?

WOMEN   850. ➤ Why are women excluded from the main
part of an Orthodox Synagogue's sitting
area during services. . . ?

ARTS &
CULTURE   851. ➤ When Elizabeth Taylor converted to Judaism, which husband was it for. . . ?

PEOPLE   852. ➤ The U.S. President who recognized Israel
was. . . ?

RELIGION   853. ➤ What is the name of the ceremony performed at the end of each Sabbath with
wine, candles and spices?

HISTORY   854. ➤ In 1917, British troops entered Jerusalem
during this Jewish holiday. . .?

LANGUAGE   855. ➤ The often-used Yiddish expression
rachmones (pronounced rahkh-moowness)
means . . .?

GEOGRAPHY 856. ➤ In 1903, English politician, Joseph
Chamberlin, suggested the creation of a
Jewish State based in this location. . .?

ANSWERS

CURRENT
EVENTS   849. ➤ *Labor* and *Likud*.

WOMEN   850. ➤ **Because they might possibly distract the mens' attention from the prayer service.**

ARTS &
CULTURE   851. ➤ **Eddie Fischer.**

PEOPLE   852. ➤ **Harry S. Truman.**

RELIGION   853. ➤ *Havdalah*.

HISTORY   854. ➤ *Chanukah*.

LANGUAGE   855. ➤ **To have compassion or understanding for someone.**

GEOGRAPHY 856. ➤ **The country that is currently known as Uganda.**

CURRENT
EVENTS   857. ➤ How many of the large Jewish communities of the world are over 100 years old. . . ?

WOMEN   858. ➤ This distinguished Israeli Premier said, "We do not rejoice in victories, we rejoice when strawberries bloom in Israel". . . ?

ARTS &
CULTURE   859. ➤ This Jewish author wrote *The Chosen* and *My Name Is Asher Lev* . . .?

PEOPLE   860. ➤ This Jewish-born Pope institutionalized celibacy for priests of the Roman Catholic Church . . .?

RELIGION 861. ➤ On what holiday is it traditional to wear white?

HISTORY   862. ➤ When the United States of America gained its independence, approximately how many Jews lived in the new nation, rounded to the nearest thousand. . .?

LANGUAGE 863. ➤ The much-used Yiddish verb *essen* means. . .?

GEOGRAPHY864. ➤ In the early 1800's, this island nation became the first British possession to grant full political emancipation to its Jewish citizens. . .?

ANSWERS

CURRENT
EVENTS   **857.** ➤ **None. All the major, large communities were destroyed during the Holocaust.**

WOMEN   **858.** ➤ **Golda Meir.**

ARTS &
CULTURE   **859.** ➤ **Chaim Potok.**

PEOPLE   **860.** ➤ **Pope Gregory.**

RELIGION   **861.** ➤ **Yom Kippur.**

HISTORY   **862.** ➤ **About 2,500. (In 1776).**

LANGUAGE **863.** ➤ **To eat.**

GEOGRAPHY **864.** ➤ **Barbados.**

Trivia Judaica   **QUESTIONS**

CURRENT
EVENTS   865. ➤ Currently, what general role does religion play in the government of Israel. . . ?

WOMEN   866. ➤ When Marilyn Monroe converted to Judaism, which husband was it for. . . ?

ARTS &
CULTURE   867. ➤ Dr. Philip Birnbaum wrote and translated many books of this type. . .?

PEOPLE   868. ➤ Dr. Chaim Weizmann, the distinguished, early Zionist, first acheived prominence as a scientist in what field. . . ?

RELIGION   869. ➤ On which holiday is a *lulav*, or willowbranch, used?

HISTORY   870. ➤ In this year, King Ferdinand ordered the Jews of Spain to either convert to Christianity or be expelled . . .?

LANGUAGE   871. ➤ What if anything is the difference between *kishka* and stuffed derma?

GEOGRAPHY   872. ➤ On May 15, 1948, name 4 of the 6 Arab armies that attacked and invaded the new State of Israel?

ANSWERS

CURRENT
EVENTS   **865.** ➤ **Religion is not seperated and influences the government. (All government offices and institutions must observe the Sabbath and all festivals.)**

WOMEN   **866.** ➤ **Arthur Miller.**

ARTS &
CULTURE   **867.** ➤ **Liturgical books (in both Hebrew and English. *The Daily Prayer Book, The High Holiday Machzor*, etc...).**

PEOPLE   **868.** ➤ **Chemistry.**

RELIGION   **869.** ➤ *Succos.*

HISTORY   **870.** ➤ **1492.**

LANGUAGE   **871.** ➤ **No difference, both mean stuffed intestines.**

GEOGRAPHY   **872.** ➤ **Those of Lebanon, Egypt, Syria, Iraq, Saudi Arabia, and Transjordan (today called Jordan).**

Trivia Judaica   **QUESTIONS**

CURRENT
EVENTS   873. ➤ They say that any two Israelis generally
              have three different opinions on any sub-
              ject, but what issue are all Israelis united
              on. . . ?

WOMEN   874. ➤ In ancient Jerusalem, this Ethiopian Queen
              came to visit a king. . . ?

ARTS &
CULTURE   875. ➤ Sid Luckman was a great _____,
              who attended this Ivy League College. . . ?

PEOPLE   876. ➤ This Jewish actor plays TV's Felix Un-
              ger. . .?

RELIGION 877. ➤ A difference between the ancient Temple
              and an ordinary synagogue is . . .?

HISTORY   878. ➤ The British called these Jewish freedom
              fighters the Stern Gang, but they were also
              known by this other name . . .?

LANGUAGE 879. ➤ The Yiddish expression *Gay feifen af' n
              yam!* means. . .?

GEOGRAPHY 880. ➤ The gold-domed Shrine of the "Bahai"
              faith is located in this Israeli city . . .?

ANSWERS

CURRENT
EVENTS **873.** ➤ **Defending themselves against a common enemy intent upon their destruction.**

WOMEN **874.** ➤ **The Queen of Sheba.**

ARTS &
CULTURE **875.** ➤ **Football Quarterback. He attended Columbia University.**

PEOPLE **876.** ➤ **Tony Randall.**

RELIGION **877.** ➤ **The Temple was in Jerusalem, Synagogues could be anywhere that Jews were located.**

HISTORY **878.** ➤ **Fighters for the Freedom of Israel or *"Lohamei Herut Yisrael"* (LEHI).**

LANGUAGE **879.** ➤ **Go whistle on the ocean.**

GEOGRAPHY **880.** ➤ **In Haifa (on Mt. Carmel).**

CURRENT
EVENTS   881. ➤ On which two fronts was Israel attacked at
the beginning of the Yom Kippur War...?

WOMEN   882. ➤ Stella Adler ran this world renowned school
...?

ARTS &
CULTURE 883. ➤ This Jewish slugger of the 1930's and
1940's had 331 career home runs, includ-
ing 11 grand slams...?

PEOPLE   884. ➤ This wealthy American Jewish family
owns, among other things, the Hyatt Hotel
chain and *McCall's Magazine*...?

RELIGION 885. ➤ This event is recalled annually in the Feast
of Lights on *Chanukah* ...?

HISTORY 886. ➤ The Western Wall was recaptured by the
Israeli Army during this month and in this
year...?

LANGUAGE 887. ➤ The Yiddish adjective *pitsel* means ...?

GEOGRAPHY 888. ➤ From what location did ships bring gold,
silver and ivory to King Solomon?

ANSWERS

CURRENT
EVENTS 881. ➤ On the Egyptian front (the Sinai), and on the Syrian front (the Golan Heights).

WOMEN 882. ➤ The Stella Adler Acting School.

ARTS &
CULTURE 883. ➤ Hank Greenberg.

PEOPLE 884. ➤ The Pritzker family of Chicago.

RELIGION 885. ➤ The triumph of Judah the Maccabee over Antiochus, in 164 C.E. (The Temple was cleansed and Jewish worship restored.)

HISTORY 886. ➤ June, 1967 (June 7th).

LANGUAGE 887. ➤ Little.

GEOGRAPHY 888. ➤ Ophir.

Trivia Judaica   **QUESTIONS**

CURRENT
EVENTS   889. ➤ What percentage of U.S. Jews live in large
                metropolitan areas (within 5% accuracy).
                . . ?

WOMEN   890. ➤ She is the most prominent Israeli femi-
                nist. . .?

ARTS &
CULTURE   891. ➤ What German Jewish born author said,
                "Where they burn books, they burn people,"
                100 years before Hitler came to power. . .?

PEOPLE   892. ➤ This Jewish psychologist and columnist
                hosted a TV talk show and wrote the book
                *What Every Woman Should Know About
                Men* . . .?

RELIGION 893. ➤ What is the main theme of the *Book of
                Lamentations*?

HISTORY   894. ➤ This religious group founded the holy cit-
                ies of Mecca and Medina . . .?

LANGUAGE 895. ➤ The Yiddish word for beautiful is . . .?

GEOGRAPHY 896. ➤ Where and what is Tiran?

ANSWERS

CURRENT
EVENTS **889.** ➤ **Ninety-Five percent.**

WOMEN **890.** ➤ **Marcia Freedman.**

ARTS &
CULTURE **891.** ➤ **Heinrich Heine.**

PEOPLE **892.** ➤ **Dr. Joyce Brothers.**

RELIGION **893.** ➤ **The destruction of Jerusalem and the unhappy implications of this for the Jewish people.**

HISTORY **894.** ➤ **The Jews.**

LANGUAGE **895.** ➤ *Shayn.*

GEOGRAPHY **896.** ➤ **A small island at the mouth of the Gulf of Eliat which controls navigation into the Red Sea. (The Egyptian blockade of the Straits of Tiran caused the 1967 Six-Day War.)**

Trivia Judaica   **QUESTIONS**

CURRENT
EVENTS   897. ➤ The International Olympic Committee supports these Israeli Olympic Games, known as. . .?

WOMEN   898. ➤ This Jewish entertainer was born Frances Rox and her trademark is her famous TV kiss . . .?

ARTS &
CULTURE   899. ➤ This widely-read author is also a rabbi and wrote *When Bad Things Happen to Good People*, and recently *To Life!* . . .?

PEOPLE   900. ➤ This member of an illustrious philanthropic American Jewish family became the first Jewish Senator in the 20th Century . . .?

RELIGION   901. ➤ Why does one chant when reading the Torah?

HISTORY   902. ➤ Adolph Hitler came to power in this year. . .?

LANGUAGE 903. ➤ The Christian world measures years according to the abbreviation A.D., meaning *Anno Domini*—while the Jewish equivalent is. . .?

GEOGRAPHY 904. ➤ French philanthropist Baron Maurice de Hirsch, suggested the creation of a Jewish state based in this location and offered to finance the emigration of Russian Jews there. . .?

ANSWERS

CURRENT
EVENTS 897. ➤ The Maccabiah Games. (They are held every four years and are open to Jewish athletes from every nation.)

WOMEN 898. ➤ Dinah Shore.

ARTS &
CULTURE 899. ➤ Harold S. Kushner.

PEOPLE 900. ➤ U.S. Senator Simon Guggenheim (elected to represent Colorado).

RELIGION 901. ➤ Because of the injunction to read the Law pleasantly.

HISTORY 902. ➤ 1933.

LANGUAGE 903. ➤ C.E. or the Common Era.

GEOGRAPHY 904. ➤ An area within Argentina.

CURRENT
EVENTS   905. ➤ In Israel, what type of court cases, if any are heard by a jury. . . ?

WOMEN   906. ➤ This Jewish female ventriloquist works with a puppet called Lambchop. . .?

ARTS &
CULTURE 907. ➤ This star of *Indiana Jones* movies is Jewish, but almost no one knows this?

PEOPLE   908. ➤ In 1967, this Israeli politician, seeking a strong leader durring the Six-Day War, publicly attempted to persuade his longtime political enemy, David Ben-Gurion, to become the Prime Minister. . .?

RELIGION 909. ➤ Name the three sections of the Bible. . .?

HISTORY 910. ➤ On March 22, 1971, 1200 Jews were arrested at a protest in Washington, D.C. What were they protesting?

LANGUAGE 911. ➤ A *Shabbos Goy* is . . .?

GEOGRAPHY 912. ➤ This large city, bordering Tel Aviv, was largely Arab prior to 1948. . .?

ANSWERS

CURRENT
EVENTS 905. ➤ **None. Israel does not have a jury system.**

WOMEN 906. ➤ **Shari Lewis.**

ARTS &
CULTURE 907. ➤ **Harrison Ford. (He never hid it , nor did he advertise it).**

PEOPLE 908. ➤ **Menachem Begin, Minister Without Portfolio .**

RELIGION 909. ➤ **The Pentateuch (Torah), the Prophets (Neviim) and the Hagiographa (Ketuvim).**

HISTORY 910. ➤ **They blocked the streets in front of the Soviet Embassy to protest the persecution of Soviet Jewry.**

LANGUAGE 911. ➤ **A gentile hired to perform tasks prohibited for Jews to do on the Sabbath.**

GEOGRAPHY 912. ➤ **Jaffa.**

Trivia Judaica   QUESTIONS

CURRENT
EVENTS   913. ➤ What two actions did Egypt take in 1967 to provoke the Six-Day War?

WOMEN   914. ➤ The character created by Shakespeare named Shylock had a daughter who was called . . .?

ARTS &
CULTURE   915. ➤ This best-selling Jewish author wrote *QB VII* . . .?

PEOPLE   916. ➤ These Jewish brothers built the largest theater empire in America, controlling at one time over 100 theaters . . .?

RELIGION   917. ➤ This religious writing is the major source of Jewish Mysticism from Medieval times to the present . . .?

HISTORY   918. ➤ Jewish immigration to Palestine was restricted in 1939 due to the British government's policy, stated in this infamous declaration . . .?

LANGUAGE 919. ➤ The radical *Hezbollah* party translates in English to . . .?

GEOGRAPHY 920. ➤ In Israel, what is 120 miles long and known as the *Araveh*. . . ?

ANSWERS

CURRENT
EVENTS 913. ➤ **They ordered all UN forces out of the Sinai and seized the Straits of Tiran with the avowed purpose of stopping all marine traffic to the major Israeli port of Eilat.**

WOMEN 914. ➤ **Jessica.**

ARTS &
CULTURE 915. ➤ **Leon Uris.**

PEOPLE 916. ➤ **The Schuberts.**

RELIGION 917. ➤ **The "*Zohar*".**

HISTORY 918. ➤ **The White Paper.**

LANGUAGE 919. ➤ **The "Party of God."**

GEOGRAPHY 920. ➤ **It is a great plain stretching from the Dead Sea to Eilat. It borders the Negev and the mountains of Jordan.**

Trivia Judaica — QUESTIONS

CURRENT
EVENTS 921. ➤ What % of Israel's land is owned by the government, within 5% accuracy. . . ?

WOMEN 922. ➤ This Jewish author wrote *Up The Down Staircase* and was the granddaughter of Sholom Aleichem . . .?

ARTS &
CULTURE 923. ➤ What award did Yehuda Amichai, the noted Israeli writer, receive in 1982?

PEOPLE 924. ➤ Which Arab President was responsible for this quote in the 1960's: "The Arab national aim is the elimination of Israel". . .?

RELIGION 925. ➤ How many versions of the Ten Commandments are there in the Bible?

HISTORY 926. ➤ What was the Russian "Black Hundred". . .?

LANGUAGE 927. ➤ This flat circular bread-like roll has an indentation in its middle and is sprinkled with flour and onion . . .?

GEOGRAPHY 928. ➤ During the American Revolution there was a company of Jewish patriot militia led by Richard Lushington, who were all residents of this southern city known for it's large early Jewish population. . . ?

ANSWERS

CURRENT
EVENTS 921. ➤ More than 90%, one of the highest rates in the world. (This is one of the reasons Israel's economy does not perform better.)

WOMEN 922. ➤ Belle Kaufman.

ARTS &
CULTURE 923. ➤ He won the Israeli Prize for Literature.

PEOPLE 924. ➤ President Nasser of Egypt (speaking to the President of Iraq and to King Hussein of Jordan).

RELIGION 925. ➤ Two (one in Exodus 20, and one in Deuteronomy 5).

HISTORY 926. ➤ The group that directed the Pogroms against Jews under the orders of the Russian government.

LANGUAGE 927. ➤ A bialy.

GEOGRAPHY 928. ➤ Charleston, South Carolina.

Trivia Judaica   QUESTIONS

CURRENT
EVENTS   929. ➤ The members of England's Parliament are called M.P.'s. What abbreviation is used for members of Israeli's Parliament. . . ?

WOMEN   930. ➤ The women's Zionist organization is better known by this other name . . .?

ARTS &
CULTURE   931. ➤ This Jewish religious ceremony began in the 14th Century, and is even more popular today among Jewish families. . . ?

PEOPLE   932. ➤ This retired, talkative Jewish sportscaster, who began his career as a lawyer, said in a recent interview with Barbara Walters, "I know that wherever I go—someone will be out to get me—because I am a Jew." . . .?

RELIGION   933. ➤ What is *Halacha* ?

HISTORY   934. ➤ Israel's secret rescue operation that airlifted the Jews of Yemen to the Jewish State was called . . .?

LANGUAGE   935. ➤ The Yiddish phrase *gehakteh tsores* refers to one who is . . .?

GEOGRAPHY 936. ➤ These two non-Middle East countries controlled the only Jewish settlements in Palestine, before Israeli statehood . . .?

ANSWERS

CURRENT
EVENTS 929. ➤ **M.K.'s (Members of Knesset).**

WOMEN 930. ➤ **Hadassah.**

ARTS &
CULTURE 931. ➤ **The *Bar Mitzvah*.**

PEOPLE 932. ➤ **Howard Cosell.**

RELIGION 933. ➤ **Jewish religious law. (Halacha deals with religious practice and observance.)**

HISTORY 934. ➤ **"Operation Magic Carpet."**

LANGUAGE 935. ➤ **In total misery.**

GEOGRAPHY936. ➤ **France and England.**

CURRENT
EVENTS   937. ➤ This American Jewish public servant won
                 the 1975 Nobel Peace Prize. . . ?

WOMEN   938. ➤ How many daughters did Tevye have in
                 Fiddler on the Roof?

ARTS &
CULTURE   939. ➤ This noted Jewish author wrote *A Beggar
                 in Jerusalem, The Golem, Night, Day* and
                 more. . . ?

PEOPLE   940. ➤ This sucessful English Jewish banker was
                 asked by British rulers to break the strangle-
                 hold that usurious Christian money lend-
                 ers had in Europe. He was knighted by
                 William III. . .?

RELIGION   941. ➤ What do the letters "KT" found on the
                 curtain which covers the Ark in a Syna-
                 gogue stand for. . .?

HISTORY   942. ➤ Which group was responsible for chang-
                 ing the name of Israel to "Palestine". . . ?

LANGUAGE   943. ➤ Survivors of the Holocaust who stayed in
                 Europe after World War II were called
                 D.P.s which means. . .?

GEOGRAPHY   944. ➤ In which geographic region in Israel do
                 most of Israel's Arab populaton reside?

ANSWERS

CURRENT
EVENTS 937. ➤ **Henry Kissinger.**

WOMEN 938. ➤ **Five.**

ARTS &
CULTURE 939. ➤ **Elie Wiesel.**

PEOPLE 940. ➤ **Solomon Medina. (His presence and money succeeded in forcing down European interest rates).**

RELIGION 941. ➤ **"*Keter Torah*" or the Crown of the Law.**

HISTORY 942. ➤ **The Romans (after they exiled the Jews).**

LANGUAGE 943. ➤ **Displaced Persons.**

GEOGRAPHY944. ➤ **The northernmost section.**

Trivia Judaica   QUESTIONS

CURRENT
EVENTS   945. ➤ Why were U.S. troops put on worldwide
               alert on October 26, 1973. . . ?

WOMEN   946. ➤ This Jewish actress played Yetta
               Marmelstein. . .?

ARTS &
CULTURE   947. ➤ These two Jewish authors wrote *The Nine
               Questions People Ask About Judaism* and
               Why The Jews . . .?

PEOPLE   948. ➤ This famous American jurist identified the
               three necessary ingredients for the realiza-
               tion of Zionism: 'Men, money and disci-
               pline" . . .?

RELIGION 949. ➤ For what holiday are candles lit near the
               Bimah by all members of the Congrega-
               tion, to memorialize their departed?

HISTORY   950. ➤ What major action, if any, did the Vatican
               take to discourage the genocide inflicted
               on the Jews during the Holocaust. . . ?

LANGUAGE 951. ➤ A *Tzaddik* is the Yiddish word for . . .?

GEOGRAPHY 952. ➤ Over the past ten years, which three Ameri-
               can cities have had the largest number of
               Soviet Jewish immigrants. . .?

ANSWERS

CURRENT
EVENTS 945. ➤ Over concern that the Soviet Union was planning to introduce its military forces into the "Yom Kippur War", aiding Egypt in their losing battle against Israel.

WOMEN 946. ➤ Barbra Streisand.

ARTS &
CULTURE 947. ➤ Joseph Telushkin and Dennis Praeger.

PEOPLE 948. ➤ U.S. Supreme Court Justice Louis Brandeis.

RELIGION 949. ➤ The Day of Atonement.

HISTORY 950. ➤ There was no intervention.

LANGUAGE 951. ➤ A righteous person, a person noted for his faith and piety.

GEOGRAPHY 952. ➤ New York City, Los Angeles, Philadelphia, Chicago, and Miami (in order of population).

Trivia Judaica   **QUESTIONS**

CURRENT
EVENTS 953. ➤ The most important natural resource of
Israel is. . . ?

WOMEN 954. ➤ This Jewish author who is also a Rabbi
wrote *Jewish Literacy*. . .?

ARTS &
CULTURE 955. ➤ This 1981 film, staring Sigourney Weaver
and William Hurt, was the first negative
portrayal of an Israeli in Hollywood history . . .?

PEOPLE 956. ➤ What did scientist Chaim Weizmann do
for the British government during World
War II which caused them to listen to his
pleas for a Zionist State?

RELIGION 957. ➤ Which act is performed during the traditional Jewish wedding ceremony to serve
as a symbolic reminder of the destruction
of the Temple?

HISTORY 958. ➤ What experience caused Theodore Herzl
to become an ardent Zionist. . . ?

LANGUAGE 959. ➤ The Yiddish expression *sitsfleisch* refers
to this quality. . . ?

GEOGRAPHY 960. ➤ Which African nation currently has the
largest Jewish population?

ANSWERS

953. ➤ The mineral wealth of the Dead Sea. (If you answer Israel's people, you've also answered this one correctly.)

WOMEN 954. ➤ Rabbi Joseph Telushkin.

ARTS &
CULTURE 955. ➤ The timing of the celebrations. The Jewish New Year's date is based on the Lunar calander and changes slightly each year, but generally comes 3 to 4 months before the secular new year.

PEOPLE 956. ➤ He invented an important chemical compound used by the British to manufacture ammunition and explosives during World War II. (This achievement opened additional political doors for him.)

RELIGION 957. ➤ The bridegroom breaks a glass with his foot.

HISTORY 958. ➤ He witnessed mobs of Frenchmen chanting "Death to the Jews" during the Dreyfus trial.

LANGUAGE 959. ➤ Perseverence, especially relating to scholarly studies.

GEOGRAPHY 960. ➤ Morocco.

Trivia Judaica   QUESTIONS

CURRENT
EVENTS   961. ➤ Cracow, Poland, had 60,000 Jews before
W. W. II. The current Jewish population is
approximately (to the nearest 100) . . .?

WOMEN   962. ➤ Except for Rachel, the Matriarchs and
Patriarchs are buried here. . . ?

ARTS &
CULTURE   963. ➤ This Israeli statesman, author and television personality wrote a recent bestselling
book which was a TV documentary. . .?

PEOPLE   964. ➤ This Jewish interviewer and newscaster is
known as the most intelligent man on
American television due to the impressive
quality of the interviews he conducts on
his evening news program . . .?

RELIGION 965. ➤ At what point during the reading of the
Purim *megillah* are congregants asked to
make noise?

HISTORY   966. ➤ The Dead Sea Scrolls were discovered
during this decade . . .?

LANGUAGE 967. ➤ Repentance, a central concept in Judaism,
applies to the believer who sins and to the
non-believer who returns. This person who
returns is known as a. . .?

GEOGRAPHY 968. ➤ The architects from the Second Temple
came from. . .?

ANSWERS

CURRENT
EVENTS   961. ➤ **200 (their average age is 73; they have no rabbi and most have had no religious education).**

WOMEN   962. ➤ **The Cave of Machpelah.**

ARTS &
CULTURE   963. ➤ **Abba Eban, the author of "*Heritage: Civilization and the Jews.*"**

PEOPLE   964. ➤ **Ted Koppel, the host of "*Nightline.*"**

RELIGION   965. ➤ **At the mention of the name of Haman.**

HISTORY   966. ➤ **The 1940's.**

LANGUAGE 967. ➤ **"*Baal Teshuvah.*"**

GEOGRAPHY 968. ➤ **Phoenicia (present day Lebanon).**

Trivia Judaica   QUESTIONS

CURRENT
EVENTS 969. ➤ This professional anti-Semite peddles racism and hate, mocks the Holocaust, calls Judaism a "gutter religion" and calls Jews "bloodsuckers" . . .?

WOMEN   970. ➤ The *Simchat Bat* refers to. . . ?

ARTS &
CULTURE 971. ➤ Jewish thinkers Abraham Joshua Heschel, Martin Buber and Franz Rosenzweig were all distinguished in this discipline . . .?

PEOPLE   972. ➤ What was Israel's "Operation Ship to Shore". . . ?

RELIGION 973. ➤ Channa and her seven sons are associated with this holiday . . .?

HISTORY 974. ➤ While the Israeli Army won the 1948 War of Independence, they sacrificed some territory during this war. What was lost?

LANGUAGE 975. ➤ The Yiddish and Ladino alphabets use these types of letters . . .?

GEOGRAPHY976. ➤ The United Nations Partition Plan of 1947 involved dividing Palestine into 3 parts under 3 areas of control. What 3 groups controlled these areas?

ANSWERS

CURRENT
EVENTS 969. ➤ **Louis Farrakhan. (More than 50% of the U.S. Black population generally approve of him, according to a February 1994 opinion poll.)**

WOMEN 970. ➤ **"The joy of having a daughter"—it is a home celebration on the Friday evening following the birth of a girl.**

ARTS &
CULTURE 971. ➤ **Philosophy.**

PEOPLE 972. ➤ **The resettlement of refugees in Israel—from their embarkation in Europe to their landing in Israel.**

RELIGION 973. ➤ **Chanukah.**

HISTORY 974. ➤ **The Jewish quarter in the Old City of Jerusalem was lost until the 1967 Six-Day War.**

LANGUAGE 975. ➤ **Hebrew.**

GEOGRAPHY 976. ➤ **The Jews controlled one zone, the Arabs another and Jerusalem was under U.N. control.**

Trivia Judaica   **QUESTIONS**

EVENTS 977. ➤ What is the name of the cancelled Israeli advanced jet fighter and what is the name of the existing Israeli manufactured supersonic jet fighter. . . ?

WOMEN 978. ➤ This Jewish female film star was known as "The Vamp" . . .?

ARTS &
CULTURE 979. ➤ The "Miracle of the Hebrew Language" refers to. . . ?

PEOPLE 980. ➤ The Jewish scholar, William F. Albright, is acknowledged to be the father of this scientific discipline. . . ?

RELIGION 981. ➤ Why did Greek and Roman slavemasters consider the Jewish people to be lazy. . . ?

HISTORY 982. ➤ In 1940, the British government allowed German Jewish refugees from the ship St. Louis-that no other nation would allow on their land-to remain in England. What was unusual about the British government's treatment of these survivors, one year later. . . ?

LANGUAGE 983. ➤ One who abandons his or her religious belief is an . . .?

GEOGRAPHY 984. ➤ These 2 Middle East nations emerged from the dismantling of the Turkish Ottoman Empire as initially French controlled areas in 1920 and independant nations in 1943 and 1944. . . ?

ANSWERS

CURRENT
EVENTS   **977.** ➤ The *Lavi* (cancelled due to discrete pressure from the U.S. government, as the plane would have had superior specifications than new U.S. planes) and the *Kfir* (in production since the early '80s).

WOMEN   **978.** ➤ Theda Bara (born Theodosia Goodman).

ARTS &
CULTURE   **979.** ➤ The survival of Hebrew as a spoken and written language, while all other ancient contemporary languages died.

PEOPLE   **980.** ➤ Archaeology.

RELIGION   **981.** ➤ Because Judaism required a day of rest for all workers.

HISTORY   **982.** ➤ They were interned as "enemy alienst" and treated as Nazi agents because they were also from Germany. The British government ignored the fact that Jews could not logically be Nazi sysmpathizers.

LANGUAGE   **983.** ➤ Apostate.

GEOGRAPHY   **984.** ➤ Syria (in 1943) and Lebanon (in 1944).

CURRENT
EVENTS   985. ➤ What was the name of the Israeli town where 21 school children were killed and 70 wounded, on May 15th, 1975. . . ?

WOMEN   986. ➤ This Jewish singer was fondly nicknamed "Bubbles." What's her real name and what was she a star of. . .?

ARTS &
CULTURE   987. ➤ This innovative Jewish teacher is known as "the father of method acting". . .?

PEOPLE   988. ➤ On January 7, 1957, this Israeli statesman said, "It is our belief that a great Jewish community, a free Jewish nation, in Palestine, with a large scope for its activities, will be of good benefit to our Arab neighbors. We need each other, we can benefit from each other". . .?

RELIGION   989. ➤ Why is a lamb bone put on the Passover table?

HISTORY   990. ➤ In 1964, what did Syria try to do vis-a-vis the Jordan River, that angered Israel?

LANGUAGE 991. ➤ The frequently used Yiddish exclamation *Genug* means . . .?

GEOGRAPHY 992. ➤ The historically accurate name for the region known as the West Bank is . .?

ANSWERS

CURRENT
EVENTS   985. ➤ Ma'alot.

WOMEN   986. ➤ Beverly Sills. She was an Opera star.

ARTS &
CULTURE   987. ➤ Lee Strasberg.

PEOPLE   988. ➤ David Ben-Gurion (responding to the findings of the Peel Commission).

RELIGION 989. ➤ To symbolize the Paschal lamb that the ancient Hebrews sacrificed before they left Egypt.

HISTORY   990. ➤ They attempted to divert the Jordan's headwaters. This would cause Israel to lose its main source of fresh water for irrigation purposes. (Israeli artillery destroyed the Syrian equipment involved in this project.)

LANGUAGE 991 ➤ Enough.

GEOGRAPHY 992 ➤ Judea and Samaria.

Trivia Judaica **QUESTIONS**

CURRENT
EVENTS 993. ➤ What was the specific Arab rationale behind the 1973 oil embargo. . .?

WOMEN 994. ➤ Her sons were humorous performers nicknamed "Minnie's Boys". . .?

ARTS &
CULTURE 995. ➤ He was the Italian Jewish painter whose trademark was painting women with long necks. . .?

PEOPLE 996. ➤ This Jewish author wrote *The Stepford Wives, Rosemary's Baby* and *The Boys From Brazil*. . .?

RELIGION 997. ➤ How many meals are traditionally required to be eaten on the Sabbath?

HISTORY 998. ➤ Of what origin or classification were the first Jews who came to America. . . ?

LANGUAGE 999. ➤ This Yiddish word refers to a person who is unlucky. It begins with the Yiddish word for luck. . .?

GEOGRAPHY 1000. ➤ Name the two Scandinavian countries where no Jews were sent to their deaths during the Nazi era. . .?

ANSWERS

CURRENT
EVENTS **993.** ➤ **They wanted the oil dependent countries to pressure Israel into returning to the 1967 cease-fire lines.**

WOMEN **994.** ➤ **The Marx Brothers.**

ARTS &
CULTURE **995.** ➤ **Modigliani.**

PEOPLE **996.** ➤ **Ira Levin.**

RELIGION **997.** ➤ **Three.**

HISTORY **998.** ➤ **Sephardic.**

LANGUAGE **999.** ➤ *"Schlimazeldiker."*

GEOGRAPHY **1000.** ➤ **Finland and Sweden.**

CURRENT
EVENTS   1001.   ➤ What was former ambassador to the U.N. Daniel Moynihan referring to when he said: "The United States will not abide by; it will not acquiesce in this infamous act. A great evil has been loosed upon the world". . .?

WOMEN   1002.   ➤ Marilyn Monroe and Elizabeth Taylor were both film stars but they also had this in common . . .?

ARTS &
CULTURE   1003.   ➤ This type of Judaism, more than any other, advocates modifications of Orthodoxy to deal with contemporary life and thought. . . ?

PEOPLE   1004.   ➤ This Jewish business wizard created the world's largest cosmetics company . . .?

RELIGION   1005.   ➤ From which direction should Chanukah candles be lit?

HISTORY   1006.   ➤ Why did Israel withdraw from the Sinai after the successful '56 Sinai Campaign?

LANGUAGE   1007.   ➤ The Hebrew word for Prayer Book is. . .?

GEOGRAPHY   1008.   ➤ The first nation to give Israel *official*, rather than *de facto* recognition was. . .?

ANSWERS

CURRENT
EVENTS **1001.** ➤ **The outrageous UN resolution condemning Zionism as a form of racism.**

WOMEN **1002.** ➤ **They converted to Judaism to marry their Jewish husbands.**

ARTS &
CULTURE **1003.** ➤ **Reform Judaism.**

PEOPLE **1004.** ➤ **Charles Revson.**

RELIGION **1005.** ➤ **Left to right.**

HISTORY **1006.** ➤ **Because the UN requested a pullback to the borders that existed before the war. (The U.S. also applied tremendous pressure forcing Israel to relinquish captured territory.)**

LANGUAGE **1007.** ➤ **"Siddur."**

GEOGRAPHY**1008.** ➤ **The Soviet Union.**

CURRENT
EVENTS   1009. ➤ What two major issues—one in poitics and one in religion—are Israelis divided on. . . ?

WOMEN   1010. ➤ *Will you still love me tomorrow*, was the refrain to one of the great hits of this Jewish singer. . .?

ARTS &
CULTURE   1011. ➤ In which area of science have the Jews made the most contribution. . . ?

PEOPLE   1012. ➤ This Jewish psychologist is known as "the father of transactional analysis". . .?

RELIGION   1013. ➤ When is the "Book of Life" inscribed, and when is it sealed?

HISTORY   1014. ➤ In response to the 1940 British restrictions on Jewish land purchases in Palestine, what Jewish leader said, "They confine the Jews within a small pale of settlement similar to that which existed in Czarist Russia . . . and as now exists only under Nazi rule?"

LANGUAGE 1015. ➤ The *Haggadah* is written in these two languages. . .?

GEOGRAPHY 1016. ➤ Name three of the six European countries in which no Jews were sent to their deaths during the Nazi era. . . ?

ANSWERS

CURRENT
EVENTS   1009.   ➤ In politics: what to do with the territories occupied since 1967. In religion:
whether or not to separate religion from
government.

WOMEN   1010.   ➤ Carole King (it was from her *Tapes-
tries* album).

ARTS &
CULTURE   1011.   ➤ Medicine.

PEOPLE   1012.   ➤ Dr. Eric Berne.

RELIGION   1013.   ➤ It is inscribed on "Rosh Hashanah,"
and sealed on "Yom Kippur."

HISTORY   1014.   ➤ David Ben-Gurion (on February 28th,
1940).

LANGUAGE   1015.   ➤ Hebrew and Aramaic.

GEOGRAPHY   1016.   ➤ Any three of these: England, Ireland,
Spain, Portugal, Albania and Switzer-
land.

CURRENT
EVENTS   1017. ➤ This Israeli Kenesset member beat the long-time Mayor of Jerusalem Teddy Kollek, in the 1993 election. What is his name and what is so unusual about the extremely busy schedule he will now have in his political life. . . ?

WOMEN   1018. ➤ These two books in the Bible are named for women. . .'?

ARTS &
CULTURE   1019. ➤ This family was a dominant force in the field of Hebrew liturgical printing for 500 years. . .?

PEOPLE   1020. ➤ This well known theologian of the Middle Ages said, "It is just as possible to convert Jews as to convert the Devil". . . ?

RELIGION   1021. ➤ The three books of the *Hagiographa* are . . .?

HISTORY   1022. ➤ Approximately what percentage of Europe's Jewish population lived in Germany up until World War II?

LANGUAGE   1023. ➤ The title *Gaon* refers to . . .?

GEOGRAPHY   1024. ➤ These two important Jewish edifices were built on Jerusalem's Mount Moriah . . .?

ANSWERS

1017. ➤ He became both Mayor of Jerusalem and a Member of Kenesset—at the same time—because he did not resign from the Kenesset, as he promised to do during his campaign. (There are some on the Kenesset committee on Kenesset Affairs who want to limit the possibility of "double allegiance" for MK's.)

WOMEN 1018. ➤ Ruth and Esther.

ARTS & CULTURE 1019. ➤ The Soncinos (the company still operates today in Europe and in the United States under different ownership).

PEOPLE 1020. ➤ Martin Luther.

RELIGION 1021. ➤ Psalms, Proverbs and Job.

HISTORY 1022. ➤ Less than 5 %.

LANGUAGE 1023. ➤ An important Rabbi.

GEOGRAPHY 1024. ➤ The First and Second Temples.

CURRENT
EVENTS   1025.   ➤ This TV talk show host invited Louis Farrakhan to appear on national TV in February of 1994 in an attempt to create controversy and boost ratings during sweeps month. . . ?

WOMEN   1026.   ➤ Centuries ago, how would the few rare female Talmudic scholars lecture to men-and still not violate the strict religious laws of their times. . . ?

ARTS &
CULTURE   1027.   ➤ The Jewish writer, Boris Pasternak, created this famous doctor in his book of the same name. . . ?

PEOPLE   1028.   ➤ This Jewish business wizard made his fortune in Canadian uranium mining and spent his money on the acquisition of art which he frequently donated to the American people. . .?

RELIGION 1029.   ➤ With which holiday is King Ahasuerus associated. . . ?

HISTORY   1030.   ➤ After World War II, a secret group called the Sonneborn Institute was formed by American Zionist Rudolf Sonneborn and others for the purpose of. . .?

LANGUAGE 1031.   ➤ The *Chanukiah* is another word for. . .?

GEOGRAPHY 1032.   ➤ Former Israeli Prime Minister Golda Meir was first a schoolteacher in this American city. . .?

ANSWERS

CURRENT
EVENTS 1025. ➤ Arsenio Hall. (He was widely condemned for this P.R. stunt.)

WOMEN 1026. ➤ They would speak from behind a closed door or from behind a screen.

ARTS &
CULTURE 1027. ➤ Doctor Zhivago.

PEOPLE 1028. ➤ Joseph P. Hirshhorn.

RELIGION 1029. ➤ Purim.

HISTORY 1030. ➤ Buying and smuggling arms and military equipment to Israel. (The formation of this clandestine American arm of the *Hagganah* was initiated by Ben-Gurion).

LANGUAGE 1031. ➤ Menorah.

GEOGRAPHY 1032. ➤ Milwaukee, Wisconsin.

Trivia Judaica   **QUESTIONS**

CURRENT
EVENTS   1033. ▶ The present Chief Rabbis of Israel pronounced these Jews as being the remnants of the Tribe of Dan . . .?

WOMEN   1034. ▶ This Jewish actress starred in a late night soap opera and was once married to Woody Allen . . .?

ARTS &
CULTURE 1035. ▶ This Jewish actor starred in the movies *Cast A Giant Shadow* and *Victory At Entebbe*. . . ?

PEOPLE   1036. ▶ What infamous company did Benjamin Siegel and Meyer Lansky found. . . ?

RELIGION 1037. ▶ On what traditional day of mourning were the Jews expelled from Spain in 1492. . . ?

HISTORY 1038. ▶ When the Nazis demanded that all Jews wear yellow identification stars, the ruler of this country wore a star himself and the entire population followed his lead, thus circumventing the Nazis, and saving many Jewish lives. . . ?

LANGUAGE 1039. ▶ Israel's national anthem *Hatikvah*, in English means. . .?

GEOGRAPHY 1040. ▶ This South American country has the highest percentage of Jews among its population . . .?

ANSWERS

CURRENT
EVENTS **1033.** ➤ **The Ethiopian Jews. (Commonly referred to as "Falashas." A pejorative term meaning strangers.)**

WOMEN **1034.** ➤ **Louise Lasser (she starred in *Mary Hartman, Mary Hartman*. He should have stayed with her given all of his latest *tsouris*).**

ARTS &
CULTURE **1035.** ➤ **Kirk Douglas.**

PEOPLE **1036.** ➤ **Murder Incorporated.**

RELIGION **1037.** ➤ *Tisha B'Av*, **the Fast of the Ninth day of** *Av*.

HISTORY **1038.** ➤ **The King of Denmark.**

LANGUAGE **1039.** ➤ **The Hope.**

GEOGRAPHY **1040.** ➤ **Uruguay (with 50,000 Jews, or 139 Jews per 1000 inhabitants).**

Trivia Judaica   **QUESTIONS**

CURRENT
EVENTS   1041.   ➤ Which organization regularly makes the rediculous claim that Jewish doctors deliberately inject the AIDS virus into Black babies. . . ?

WOMEN   1042.   ➤ This Jewish actress was the heroine of *Star Wars*. . .?

ARTS &
CULTURE   1043.   ➤ This Israeli literary prize is awarded to the author who best expresses the idea of freedom of the individual in society. . .?

PEOPLE   1044.   ➤ This rabbi was immortalized in a famous Rembrandt etching. . .?

RELIGION   1045.   ➤ What book from the Apocrypha relates the story of *Chanukah*. . . ?

HISTORY   1046.   ➤ This American President appointed the first Jew to the U.S. Supreme Court. . .?

LANGUAGE   1047.   ➤ The derisive Hebrew term *Yekkee* refers to this type of Jew. . .?

GEOGRAPHY 1048.   ➤ This nation is Israel's second largest export partner. . .?

ANSWERS

CURRENT
EVENTS   **1041.** ➤ The nation of Islam (led by arch-anti-Semite Louis Farrakhan).

WOMEN   **1042.** ➤ Carrie Fisher (daughter of Eddie Fisher and Debbie Reynolds).

ARTS &
CULTURE   **1043.** ➤ The Jerusalem Prize.

PEOPLE   **1044.** ➤ Rabbi Manassah Ben Israel.

RELIGION   **1045.** ➤ The Book of Maccabees.

HISTORY   **1046.** ➤ Woodrow Wilson.

LANGUAGE **1047.** ➤ One of German ethnic background. (It is often used pejoratively to describe one who is very rigid.)

GEOGRAPHY **1048.** ➤ West Germany.

Trivia Judaica   **QUESTIONS**

CURRENT
EVENTS   1049.   ➤ The disputed remains of this long-sought Nazi were found in Embo, Brazil in 1985 . . .?

WOMEN   1050.   ➤ This female Jewish author influenced literary and artistic life of the 1920's and 1930's. Her best known work was the *Autobiography of Alice B. Toklas*. . .?

ARTS &
CULTURE   1051.   ➤ This Jewish intellectual owns and publishes *The New Republic* magazine?

PEOPLE   1052.   ➤ This distinguished Jewish author taught at Sarah Lawrence College and wrote *Ragtime*, *The Book of Daniel*, *Worlds Fair* and *Billy Bathgate*. . .?

RELIGION   1053.   ➤ What is the major distinction that Reform Judaism makes concerning Jewish Law?

HISTORY   1054.   ➤ He was the first early American Jewish leader to demand equal rights for the Jewish people in the newly emancipated colonies . . .?

LANGUAGE   1055.   ➤ The German term *Judenrein*, used frequently during the Holocaust, means . . .?

GEOGRAPHY   1056.   ➤ Israel destroyed the P.L.O. headquaters in a long-distance raid in this nation, after 3 Israelis were murdered aboard their yacht in Larcana, Cyprus. . .?

ANSWERS

CURRENT
EVENTS **1049.** ➤ Dr. Joseph Mengele (also known as Auschwitz's Angel of Death).

WOMEN **1050.** ➤ Gertrude Stein.

ARTS &
CULTURE **1051.** ➤ Martin Peretz (a descendent of I.L. Peretz).

PEOPLE **1052.** ➤ E. L. Doctorow.

RELIGION **1053.** ➤ It emphasizes the Laws which have a universal ethical importance and minimizes the importance of those that apply to particular times and conditions.

HISTORY **1054.** ➤ Asser Levy. (He was active in New Amsterdam, now New York City.)

LANGUAGE **1055.** ➤ Free of any Jews.

GEOGRAPHY **1056.** ➤ Tunisia. (In October 1985, Israeli fighter jets flew 1500 miles and decimated the P.L.O.'s world headquarters. This was Israel's most long-range military mission since the Entebbe rescue mission of 1976 and the Iraq reactor attack of 1981.)

CURRENT
EVENTS   1057. ➤ In 1994, Israel's Foreign Prime Minister Shimon Peres told this noted Arab terrorist, "Don't adorn yourself with someone else's feathers. Today you are an ex-terrorist". . . ?

WOMEN   1058. ➤ What Biblical figure does the women's group *Hadassah* take it's name from. . . ?

ARTS &
CULTURE   1059. ➤ What are the three major names the Bible uses to refer to the Jews. . . ?

PEOPLE   1060. ➤ This Jewish singer wrote a famous song about a restaurant where one could "get anything you want". . . ?

RELIGION   1061. ➤ On which holiday is the ceremony of *Tashlich* performed, in which one's sins are symbolically cast away?

HISTORY   1062. ➤ The Jewish period of prosperity in Spain became known as. . . ?

LANGUAGE 1063. ➤ After Israel, the second most active Yiddish population center is . . .?

GEOGRAPHY 1064. ➤ When, if ever, was Jerusalem the capital city of an Arab country. . . ?

ANSWERS

CURRENT
EVENTS 1057. ➤ **Yassar Arafat. (Peres made this incredible comment to him after signing the Israeli-PLO accord in Cairo, in February 1994, according to published reports.)**

WOMEN 1058. ➤ **Esther. (*Hadassah* is the Hebrew form of the Persian name Esther).**

ARTS &
CULTURE 1059. ➤ **Jews, Israelites, and Hebrews.**

PEOPLE 1060. ➤ **Arlo Guthrie (*Alice's Restaurant*).**

RELIGION 1061. ➤ *Rosh Hashanah.*

HISTORY 1062. ➤ **The Golden Age.**

LANGUAGE 1063. ➤ **Buenos Aires, Argentina.**

GEOGRAPHY 1064. ➤ **Never.**

Trivia Judaica　　　QUESTIONS

CURRENT
EVENTS　1065.　➤ What did Croatian President Franjo Tudjman do in early 1994, when he learned sections of a book he wrote were perceived to be anti-Semitic and offensive to Jews around the world. . . ?

WOMEN　1066.　➤ The Yiddish food made by frying crushed matzahs that are mixed together with eggs and milk is called. . . ?

ARTS &
CULTURE　1067.　➤ What event inspired Shakespeare to write *The Merchant Of Venice*. . . ?

PEOPLE　1068.　➤ This American Zionist was Treasury Secretary from 1934 to 1945, when he resigned to devote himself exclusively to Jewish affairs . . .?

RELIGION　1069.　➤ Haman, the villain of the Purim story, had how many sons?

HISTORY　1070.　➤ Adolph Cremieux, a famous Jewish French statesman from 1840 to 1880, successfully led a life-long fight for this. . .?

LANGUAGE 1071.　➤ In Yiddish, when a person receives a *zetz*, they get a . . .?

GEOGRAPHY 1072.　➤ What country is Northeast of Israel. . . ?

ANSWERS

CURRENT
EVENTS   **1065.** ➤ **He apologized to the American Jewish community through a public letter to the Anti-Defamation League of B'nai B'rith.**

WOMEN   **1066.** ➤ *Matzah Brie.* **(Served either scrambled or in the form of a fried or baked pie.)**

ARTS &
CULTURE   **1067.** ➤ **The execution of a Portuguese Jew, Rodrigo Lopez, who was accused of treason.**

PEOPLE   **1068.** ➤ **Henry Morgenthau, Jr.**

RELIGION   **1069.** ➤ **Ten.**

HISTORY   **1070.** ➤ **The fight for equal treatment for the Jews of France (and Jews all over the world).**

LANGUAGE   **1071.** ➤ **Punch .**

GEOGRAPHY   **1072.** ➤ **Syria.**

CURRENT
EVENTS   1073.   ➤ What did the Arab league do in early
1994, to shock and dismay the Conference
of Presidents of Major American Jewish
Organizations. . . ?

WOMEN   1074.   ➤ This Jewish woman was a Biblical
judge. . . ?

ARTS &
CULTURE   1075.   ➤ The Black Jews of Ethiopia call themselves by what name. . . ?

PEOPLE   1076.   ➤ Which British statesman said "I hope
that . . . they will not grudge that small
notch—for it is no more than that geo-
graphically, whatever it may be historically—in what are now Arab territories,
being given to the people who for all these
hundreds of years have been separated
from it. . . ?"

RELIGION   1077.   ➤ This Book of the Bible is read during
the *Tisha B'Av* service. . .?

HISTORY   1078.   ➤ When and for how long did the Warsaw
Ghetto Uprising occur. . . ?

LANGUAGE   1079.   ➤ The Hebrew word for "light" is. . . ?

GEOGRAPHY   1080.   ➤ The only city in Nebraska with over
1,000 Jewish residents is . . .?

ANSWERS

CURRENT
EVENTS 1073. ➤ They renegged on a committment they had made to place the ending of the secondary boycott of Israel on the agenda of their 1994 meeting.

WOMEN 1074. ➤ Deborah.

ARTS &
CULTURE 1075. ➤ *Beta-Israel.* (Literally, House of Israel.)

PEOPLE 1076. ➤ A.J. Balfour (July 12th, 1920).

RELIGION 1077. ➤ The Book of Lamentations.

HISTORY 1078. ➤ In 1943, for 28 days.

LANGUAGE 1079. ➤ *"Ohr."*

GEOGRAPHY 1080. ➤ Omaha. (An estimated 6,500 live there. Lincoln is next with approximately 800.)

Trivia Judaica   **QUESTIONS**

CURRENT
EVENTS   1081.   ➤ The "Mastif" and "Scout" are the names
                     of a sophisticated weapon that Israel is
                     exporting. This weapon is . . .?

WOMEN   1082.   ➤ This female Jewish scientist won a
                     Nobel prize for her medical research. . . ?

ARTS &
CULTURE   1083.   ➤ *Rabbi Ben Ezra* was a poem written by
                     this famous non-Jewish poet. . . ?

PEOPLE   1084.   ➤ This Jewish U.S. Supreme Court Jus-
                     tice was known as "The People's Attor-
                     ney" . . .?

RELIGION   1085.   ➤ *Lag. B'Omer* occurs how many days
                     into the counting of the omen?

HISTORY   1086.   ➤ He was the Jewish Secretary of State in
                     the days of the Confederacy. . .?

LANGUAGE   1087.   ➤ The British government gave this title
                     to the British-appointed ruler of Palestine
                     during the Mandate period . . .?

GEOGRAPHY   1088.   ➤ Canada's growing Jewish community
                     now numbers . . .?

ANSWERS

CURRENT
EVENTS **1081.** ➤**Drone aircraft used for pilotless re-connaissance missions.**

WOMEN **1082.** ➤**Rosalyn Yalow (in 1977).**

ARTS &
CULTURE **1083.** ➤**Robert Browning.**

PEOPLE **1084.** ➤**Louis D. Brandeis.**

RELIGION **1085.** ➤**Thirty-three days.**

HISTORY **1086.** ➤**Judah P. Benjamin.**

LANGUAGE **1087.** ➤**High Commissioner.**

GEOGRAPHY**1088.** ➤**Approximately 400,000.**

CURRENT
EVENTS   1089.   ➤ This Israeli political party believes that Israel has a Biblical obligation to retain the West Bank territories ?

WOMEN   1090.   ➤ This Sabbath delicacy is often called "Jewish Soul food". . .?

ARTS &
CULTURE   1091.   ➤ This Jewish comedian's penchant is to insult people in the audience with his quick sardonic wit. He recently also had his own sit-com in 1994, where he moved in with his son. . .?

PEOPLE   1092.   ➤ What did Jonas Salk and Albert Sabin discover. . .?

RELIGION   1093.   ➤ A food that is neither meat nor dairy is called. . .?

HISTORY   1094.   ➤ The Sykes-Picot Agreement accepted by these two European nations, was the basis for the future of the Palestine area. . .?

LANGUAGE 1095.   ➤ The Yiddish expression *Shanda* means . . .?

GEOGRAPHY 1096.   ➤ This range of hills divides Israel and Syria. . . ?

ANSWERS

CURRENT
EVENTS 1089. ➤ "Gush Emunim."

WOMEN 1090. ➤ *Cholent.*

ARTS &
CULTURE 1091. ➤ Don Rickles.

PEOPLE 1092. ➤ The Polio vaccine.

RELIGION 1093. ➤ *"Parve."*

HISTORY 1094. ➤ Britain and France.

LANGUAGE 1095. ➤ A shame, a scandal or an embarrassment.

GEOGRAPHY 1096. ➤ Golan Heights.

Trivia Judaica   **QUESTIONS**

CURRENT
EVENTS   1097.   ➤ During the Yom Kippur War how close to Damascus did Israeli forces get (with 5 miles accuracy) . . .?

WOMEN   1098.   ➤ This leading Jewish feminist leader was once a Playboy bunny . . .?

ARTS &
CULTURE   1099.   ➤ This Jewish actor was the star of *Spartacus* . . .?

PEOPLE   1100.   ➤ This man had come to be known as the "Jewish Farrakhan". . .?

RELIGION   1101.   ➤ A *mezuzah* should always be placed on this side of the doorpost . . .?

HISTORY   1102.   ➤ What precipitated the Israel-Egyptian fighting in the Sinai, during 1956?

LANGUAGE   1103.   ➤ The derogatory Yiddish term *Shmatta* refers to something that is. . .?

GEOGRAPHY   1104.   ➤ The notorious Auschwitz concentration camp was in this country. . .?

ANSWERS

CURRENT
EVENTS 1097. ➤ 25 miles.

WOMEN 1098. ➤ Gloria Steinem.

ARTS &
CULTURE 1099 ➤ Kirk Douglas.

PEOPLE 1100. ➤ Former Knesset member Meir Kahane for his outspoken extremist position and his racist political views.

RELIGION 1101. ➤ The right side.

HISTORY 1102. ➤ Egypt sealed the Israeli port of Eilat by blocking the Gulf of Aqaba, preventing the movement of Israeli shipping. Israel regarded this an act act of war.

LANGUAGE 1103. ➤ Cheap or junk.

GEOGRAPHY 1104. ➤ Poland.

Trivia Judaica QUESTIONS

CURRENT
EVENTS 1105. ➤ What did France's Defense Minister do in February, 1994 when the Chief of the Army's history section published a report that cast doubt on the innocence of Captain Alfred Dreyfus. . . ?

WOMEN 1106. ➤ What female author wrote a best-selling *Roman a clef* about her disasterous marriage to this Jewish Watergate sleuth?

ARTS &
CULTURE 1107. ➤ This Jewish writer is one of the most widely read social and political satirists today. He highlights the ridiculousness of the American way of life in his columns and books. . . ?

PEOPLE 1108. ➤ What was the reaction of Lord Moyne, Britain's Middle East Minister, to Adolph Eichmann's offer to trade 100,000 Jews for trucks, soap and coffee. . . ?

RELIGION 1109. ➤ This Jewish scholar had not studied until the age of 40 when his wife urged him to go off and learn the *Torah*. He returned 24 years later with 24,000 disciples. . .?

HISTORY 1110. ➤ There were no synagogues built in Spain for how many hundreds of years. . . ?

LANGUAGE 1111. ➤ The not-so-nice Yiddish expression *Alter kocker* means . . .?

GEOGRAPHY 1112. ➤ The capital of the ancient Jewish kingdom of Judea was . . .?

ANSWERS

CURRENT
EVENTS   1105.   ➤ He immediately fired the historian.
(France's Defense Minister, Francois
Leotard, is an open friend of the Jewish
Community and of Israel.)

WOMEN   1106.   ➤ Nora Ephron, the novel is
"*Heartburn*," her former husband is Carl
Bernstein.

ARTS &
CULTURE   1107.   ➤ Art Buchwald.

PEOPLE   1108.   ➤ He turned down the offer stating, "A
hundred thousand Jews! What am I to
do with them? Where am I to put them?"

RELIGION   1109.   ➤ Rabbi Akiva.

HISTORY   1110.   ➤ 600 Years.

LANGUAGE   1111.   ➤ Old fogey or old man.

GEOGRAPHY   1112.   ➤ Jerusalem.

281

Trivia Judaica — QUESTIONS

CURRENT
EVENTS 1113. ➤ The most sucessful commercial film maker in history has been scheduled by the Academy numerous times, but in 1994, this Jewish creative genius finally got his just due. What is his name, what was his 1994 movie called and how many nominations did it receive. . . ?

WOMEN 1114. ➤ This Jewish movie star and singer endowned a chair in Jewish studies in her father's name at a leading American university . . .?

ARTS &
CULTURE 1115. ➤ This famous gentile artist portrayed Moses holding the two tablets in a world-renowned painting. . .?

PEOPLE 1116. ➤ This Israeli anthropologist is the author of *Masada Bar Kochba*, *Hazor* and several books on the Dead Sea Scrolls . . .?

RELIGION 1117. ➤ Which Biblical Book involves the delivery of the Jewish people from slavery, their acceptance of the Covenant and their receiving the Law. . .?

HISTORY 1118. ➤ The Jews of Berlin formally dedicated their first synagogue in this century. . . ?

LANGUAGE 1119. ➤ What is the *Kol Yisroel*. . . ?

GEOGRAPHY 1120. ➤ What is ironic about the misnomers Dead Sea and Sea of Galilee. . .?

ANSWERS

CURRENT
EVENTS   **1113.** ➤ Steven Speilberg, the movie was *Schindler's List* and it received 12 nominations.

WOMEN   **1114.** ➤ Barbra Streisand.

ARTS &
CULTURE   **1115.** ➤ Rembrandt.

PEOPLE   **1116.** ➤ Professor Yigael Yadin.

RELIGION   **1117.** ➤ The Book of Exodus.

HISTORY   **1118.** ➤ The Eighteenth (1712).

LANGUAGE   **1119.** ➤ The Israel radio service.

GEOGRAPHY   **1120.** ➤ The Dead Sea is actually a large salt water lake and the Sea of Galilee is really a large fresh water lake.

Trivia Judaica   **QUESTIONS**

CURRENT
EVENTS   1121.   ➤ Even though the area in question is only a few thousand square yards! Taba is very important to Israel and Egypt because . . .?

WOMEN   1122.   ➤ This Jewish writer wrote the smash movie *Sleepless In Seattle* . . .?

ARTS &
CULTURE   1123.   ➤ He is sometimes referred to as the "Jewish Mark Twain" because of the stories he wrote . . .?

PEOPLE   1124.   ➤ This prominent American Reform Jewish leader purposely kept the news of the Holocaust hidden from American Jewry for many months . . .?

RELIGION 1125.   ➤ Jewish religious law requires that a husband write and deliver a bill of divorce to his wife in order for the marriage to be terminated. A Jewish divorce is called a . . .?

HISTORY   1126.   ➤ Uriah P. Levy, a Jewish Captain in the United States Navy is noted in history for this humanitarian accomplishment. . . ?

LANGUAGE 1127.   ➤ What does the name *Abraham* mean?

GEOGRAPHY 1128.   ➤ Haifa is in this direction from Tel Aviv . . .?

ANSWERS

CURRENT
EVENTS **1121.** ➤ It is valuable waterfront land on which Israeli developers had spent tens of millions of dollars developing major resort hotels. (Egypt now controls the land, but the tourists don't come as they used to when Israel owned it.)

WOMEN **1122.** ➤ Nora Ephron.

ARTS &
CULTURE **1123.** ➤ Sholom Aleichem.

PEOPLE **1124.** ➤ Rabbi Stephen S. Wise. (He was asked by the U.S. government to suppress the news he had heard from the World Jewish Congress until it could be verified by the U.S. State Department.)

RELIGION **1125.** ➤ *A get.*

HISTORY **1126.** ➤ He was responsible for the abolishment of corporal punishment in the U.S. Navy.

LANGUAGE **1127.** ➤ Father of many.

GEOGRAPHY **1128.** ➤ North.

Trivia Judaica   **QUESTIONS**

CURRENT
EVENTS 1129. ▶ The controversial 1982 War in Lebanon cost Israel how many lives (within 10% accuracy) . . .?

WOMEN 1130. ▶ *A Spy for Freedom*, a book by Irene Gunther and Ida Cohen, is the true story of this Jewish heroine . . .?

ARTS &
CULTURE 1131. ▶ He directed the movie *Sleepless In Seattle* and was also immortalized in his role as a "meat head". . .?

PEOPLE 1132. ▶ This Zionist leader used the pen name *Altalena*. . .?

RELIGION 1133. ▶ Jewish law forbids the drinking of this liquid. . .?

HISTORY 1134. ▶ This British statesman said on February 8, 1920: "If there should be a Jewish State under the protection of the British Crown . . . an event will have occurred in the history of the world which would . . . be beneficial, and would be especially in harmony with the truest interests of the British Empire. . .?

LANGUAGE 1135. ▶ The uncomplimentary term "Safe Jew" refers to this type of Jewish person. . . ?

GEOGRAPHY 1136. ▶ The Simon Wiesenthal Center for Holocaust Studies is located in . . .?

ANSWERS

CURRENT
EVENTS **1129.** ▶ **654 (with 3,840 wounded).**

WOMEN **1130.** ▶ **Sarah Aaronsohn.**

ARTS &
CULTURE **1131.** ▶ **Rob Reiner.**

PEOPLE **1132.** ▶ **Vladamir Ze'ev Jabotinsky.**

RELIGION **1133.** ▶ **Blood.**

HISTORY **1134.** ▶ **Winston Churchill.**

LANGUAGE **1135.** ▶ **One whose ethnic blandness makes him or her all but invisible as a Jew.**

GEOGRAPHY **1136.** ▶ **Los Angeles, California.**

Trivia Judaica **QUESTIONS**

CURRENT
EVENTS   1137. ➤ Why has the Muslim world condemned the Vatican for recognizing Israel. . . ?

WOMEN   1138. ➤ What is the name of the Amencan movie about the life of Golda Meir and who played Golda. . .?

ARTS &
CULTURE   1139. ➤ Eliezer Ben Yehuda was a noted scholar in this area of research. . .?

PEOPLE   1140. ➤ Name two Jewish major league baseball players in the Baseball Hall of Fame. . .?

RELIGION   1141. ➤ What are inside *Tefillin*?

HISTORY   1142. ➤ He was born in the 10th Century with the name Sholmo Ben Isaac and became the most renowned Bible commentator . . .?

LANGUAGE   1143. ➤ In Yiddish one who is *shluffedik* is. . .?

GEOGRAPHY   1144. ➤ Napoleon was defeated and Moshe Dayan imprisoned in this same city in Palestine. . .?

ANSWERS

CURRENT
EVENTS   1137.   ➤ Because they believe the Christian West is allying itself with Zionism against the Arabs and Muslims.

WOMEN   1138.   ➤ "Golda," starring Ingrid Bergman. (It was also a play starring Anne Bancroft.)

ARTS &
CULTURE   1139.   ➤ Language (*Ben Yehuda's Dictionary*).

PEOPLE   1140.   ➤ Hank Greenberg and Sandy Koufax.

RELIGION   1141.   ➤ Quotations from Exodus and Deuteronomy that are hand lettered in Hebrew on a small piece of paper.

HISTORY   1142.   ➤ History.

LANGUAGE   1143.   ➤ Sleepy or dull.

GEOGRAPHY   1144.   ➤ Acre.

Trivia Judaica QUESTIONS

CURRENT
EVENTS 1145. ➤ What is the main reason for the Arab's new willingness to make peace in the 1990's. . . ?

WOMEN 1146. ➤ She wrote the Jewish bestseller: *How to Run a Traditional Jewish Household. . .*?

ARTS &
CULTURE 1147. ➤ This Jewish author won the 1958 Nobel Prize in Literature. . .?

PEOPLE 1148. ➤ This American President said: "Americans agree that in Palestine shall be laid the foundations of a Jewish commonwealth". . .?

RELIGION 1149. ➤ This Jewish Sage was sometimes referred to as the "Second Moses" . . .?

HISTORY 1150. ➤ What paramilitary organization did David Raziel and Abraham Stern form in 1938 before the creation of Israel. . . ?

LANGUAGE 1151. ➤ The Yiddish words *Chazzen, Chazzer* and *Chazzerai* translate into these English words. . . ?

GEOGRAPHY 1152. ➤ Anne Frank lived in this city . . .?

ANSWERS

CURRENT
EVENTS **1145.** ➤ The collapse of their main arms and financial supporter, the Soviet Union.

WOMEN **1146.** ➤ Blu Greenberg.

ARTS &
CULTURE **1147.** ➤ Boris Leonidovich Pasternak.

PEOPLE **1148.** ➤ Woodrow Wilson.

RELIGION **1149.** ➤ Moses Maimonides.

HISTORY **1150.** ➤ The *Irgun Zvie Leumi* or National Military Organization. (They were in the Revisionist party.)

LANGUAGE **1151.** ➤ Cantor, pig, trash.

GEOGRAPHY **1152.** ➤ Amsterdam.

CURRENT
EVENTS   1153.   ➤ This industry today is Israel's largest
                  employer with some 60,000 workers (al-
                  most 20% of the labor force) engaged in
                  150 plants. . . ?

WOMEN   1154.   ➤ This Biblical figure is the symbol of
                  distrust in women. . . ?

ARTS &
CULTURE   1155.   ➤ This Jewish composer and trumpeteer
                  is well known for his 1960's Mexican-style
                  band. . . ?

PEOPLE   1156.   ➤ This notorious war criminal was tried
                  in Jerusalem in 1961. . . ?

RELIGION 1157.   ➤ On this Jewish holiday it is customary
                  to eat a dairy meal . . . ?

HISTORY   1158.   ➤ When Chaim Weizmann took office as
                  Israel's first president, what was he forced
                  to relinquish . . . ?

LANGUAGE 1159.   ➤ When one is Frank he or she is . . . ?

GEOGRAPHY 1160.   ➤ This is the only Arab country where
                  Jews enjoy full equallity and the Jewish
                  community has full recognition . . . ?

ANSWERS

CURRENT
EVENTS 1153. ➤ The arms industry.

WOMEN 1154. ➤ Jezebel. (She was the Phonecian wife of King Ahab.)

ARTS &
CULTURE 1155. ➤ Herb Albert.

PEOPLE 1156. ➤ Adolph Eichmann.

RELIGION 1157. ➤ *Shavuos.*

HISTORY 1158. ➤ His British citizenship.

LANGUAGE 1159. ➤ Ill

GEOGRAPHY 1160. ➤ Morocco. (King Hassan II is only anti-Semitic in his rhetoric, not his actions.)

Trivia Judaica   **QUESTIONS**

CURRENT
EVENTS   1161.   ➤ The members of this anti-Semitic U.S. organization are commonly referred to as *Black Nazis*. . . ?

WOMEN   1162.   ➤ This famous Jewish Biblical figure won a beauty contest and then a kingdom. . . ?

ARTS &
CULTURE   1163.   ➤ Jewish publisher Bennett Cerf, founded this major U.S. publishing firm . . . ?

PEOPLE   1164.   ➤ What device was Jewish scientist Edward Teller connected with. . . ?

RELIGION 1165.   ➤ This Talmudic figure is referred to as the "Jewish Rip Van Winkle" because he slept for 700 years . . . ?

HISTORY   1166.   ➤ On Nov. 30th 1947, what was the Syrian Delegate to the UN referring to when he made this speech stating: "Arabs and Moslems throughout the world will obstruct it, and all Asia with its thousand million people will oppose it"?

LANGUAGE 1167.   ➤ "The day is _____, the task is _____?" The missing words are. . .?

GEOGRAPHY 1168.   ➤ Raoul Wallenberg rescued tens of thousands of Jews mostly from this nation. . .?

ANSWERS

CURRENT
EVENTS 1161. ➤ **The nation of Islam.**

WOMEN 1162. ➤ **Queen Esther.**

ARTS &
CULTURE 1163. ➤ **Random House.**

PEOPLE 1164. ➤ **The Hydrogen bomb.**

RELIGION 1165. ➤ **Honi ha Meagel.**

HISTORY 1166. ➤ **The U.N. Partition Plan of Palestine. (This speech occurred the day after the UN announcement.)**

LANGUAGE 1167. ➤ **Short, great.**

GEOGRAPHY 1168. ➤ **Hungary.**

Hot New Titles of Jewish Interest From S.P.I.

Great S.P.I Books
Fact And Fiction

☐ **The Super Swindlers: The Incredible Record of America's Greatest Financial Scams** *by Jonathan Kwitney.* They say that crime doesn't pay, but it has paid quite handsomely, thank you, for some of America's greatest swindlers and con-men. Acclaimed investigative journalist Jonathan Kwitney (The *Wall Street Journal, The Kwitney Report*—PBS TV) tracks down these notorious paper pirates who have taken individuals, corporations and governments to the cleaners. In The Super Swindlers we find out how these con-men have been operating and how so many of them have avoided prosecution. (ISBN 1-56171-248-5) $5.99 U.S.

☐ **First Hand Knowledge: How I Participated In The CIA-Mafia Murder of President Kennedy** *by Robert D. Morrow.* We still have far more questions than facts about that dark November day in Dallas. But now out of the shadows, comes the only inner-circle operative not to have been mysteriously assassinated. The author's information was the basis of the House Select committee on Assassinations 1976 investigation. Morrow finally feels the danger to himself and his family passed and he is ready to talk. (ISBN 1-56171-274-4) $5.99 U.S.

☐ **Love Before The Storm: A True Romance Saga in the Shadow Of The Third Reich** *by Roslyn Tanzman.* They were two young Jewish medical students, in love, and studying medicine in Europe's greatest medical schools. The future looked rosy, until the German economy tottered and the right-wing forces marched into power. In this moving, true retelling of her parents' actual love story, Roslyn Tanzman recreates their love at first sight, their class-war between the family and the shadow cast upon the lovers by Hitler's Germany and impending World War.
(ISBN 1-56171-240-X) $5.50 U.S.

Terrorism Against Israel and The United States

BOOKS

☐ **What Am I Eating? Facts Everyone Should Know About Foods by Dr. Mia Parsonet.** An all-purpose handbook designed to provide easy-to-understand, practical information about all the foods and vitamins we consume. Contains clear and concise answers to questions concerning food and nutrition, including: are fast foods really so bad? Are health foods really so healthy? Is it wise to use bottled water? What is the record of vitamin supplements? Dr. Parsonnet has compiled an essential handbook for anyone concerned about their diet. (ISBN 1-56171-034-2) $12.95 U.S.

☐ **Stop The Nonsense: Health Without the Fads by Dr. Ezra Soher.** For everyone confused by the newest fads and "latest" discoveries about what's good for us and what's not, this book cuts through the clutter and delivers the straight facts. Dr. Sohar calls upon us to develop a logical, "life-style approach" to good health based on solid scientific evidence, reducing the confusion from the latest, often contradictory, medical advice. "...Offers a common sense approach to health and nutrition...contrasts favorably with all the recently promulgated fads on dieting." — Jean Mayer, President, Tufts University, Chairman (fmr), White House Conference on Nutrition and Health. (ISBN 1-56171-006-7) $16.95 U.S.

☐ **Who Said That? Outrageous Celebrity Quotes by Ronald L. Smith.** Here is the largest collection of memorable quotes from America's top pop icons, stars of the big screen, the small screen, the music scene and more. Readers are challenged to identify the sources of unforgettable quotes. (ISBN 1-56171-228-0) $4.99 U.S.
